Dear Iain & Lou

Than [barcode] !

DRIVEN to ACHIEVE

For all we achieved together :)

Nikki x

© 2025, Nikki Butlin, Stronger As A Team Publishing

All rights reserved

No part of this publication may be reproduced, distributed, or transmitted in any form or by any means, including photocopying, recording, or other electronic or mechanical methods, without the prior written permission of the author/publisher, except in the case of brief quotations embodied in critical reviews and certain other non-commercial uses permitted by copyright law. For permission requests, write to the author/publisher, addressed "Attention: Permissions Coordinator," at the address below.

Stronger As A Team Publishing is a trading name of
Stronger As A Team Ltd.
Registered in England & Wales No. 16278312
3rd Floor, 86–90 Paul Street, London

Cover photograph by Toby Lee
headshottoby.co.uk

Cover design by Simon Clements
simonclementscreative.co.uk

Typeset by The Book Typesetters
thebooktypesetters.com

Paperback ISBN: 978-1-0684435-0-3
eBook ISBN: 978-1-0684435-1-0

DRIVEN *to* ACHIEVE

TRANSFORMING CHALLENGES INTO OPPORTUNITIES

NIKKI BUTLIN

For Dad

My first business mentor and sounding board, who taught me that hard work and determination pays off.

Though I cannot see you anymore, I hear your voice every day.

X

For Hannah

I work hard to show you the way.

The future is bright for you my darling.

#MummaKnows

Disclaimer

This book is based on the author's personal experiences, observations and opinions, developed over a career in business. The views expressed are those of the author and do not reflect the opinions of any past or present employers, clients or associates. This book is not intended to provide legal, financial, or professional advice. Readers should seek appropriate counsel relevant to their own business circumstances.

Contents

Foreword	11
About This Book	14
Who Am I?	16
Building Character	**19**
Childhood Initiative	22
Break A Leg (or an arm)!	28
Bailing Out of Sixth Form	32
Finding Love Take #1	35
Singing	37
Motherhood	43
Hypnotherapy	50
Franchising	55
Sink or Swim	61
Set Up, Grow & Scale	**63**
The Family Firm	64
Gifts 4U UK	72
Athena Business Services	76
My Daughter's Story	83

Get Your Voice Heard — 87
    We're Getting the Band Back Together — 88
    No Boys Allowed! — 89
    4Networking & Brad Burton — 92
    Captain Fawcett — 100

Team Is Everything — 113
    Joining ASC Metals — 115
    Richard's Story — 124
    Work Yourself Out First — 127
    Build the Gaps Around You — 129
    Keys to Recruiting — 133
    People Issues — 135

Money! Money! Money! — 137
    Keep Your House in Order — 138
    Numbers Tell a Story — 140
    Cash Flow Mastery — 143
    Pay Your Bills on Time, Every Time — 147
    Be Honest with Everyone — 149
    Don't Put Your Head in the Sand — 151

Lessons Learned — 153
    I've Quit Numerous Times — 154
    No One Can Take Away Your Skills — 156
    Trust Your Instincts — 158
    Don't Focus on the Competition — 160
    Confidence — 162
    What Someone Else Thinks of You… — 164
    Keep Getting Back Up Again — 167
    Moving On Is Ok — 170
    No One Will Talk About Your Ironing at Your Funeral! — 173
    Treat Your Goals Like Car Journeys — 175

Drive, Walk, Shower!	178
Keep Making Positive Plans	180
Tunnel Vision for the Win	184
Know What You Sell and to Who	187
Know Where to Communicate	190
Rapport, Trust & Integrity	193
Sales Funnel	196
Make It Easy for People to Say Yes	198
No Hard Sell	200
Upsell	202
Work/Life Balance	205
You'll Know When You're on the Right Path	207
Celebrate Your Wins	209
Enjoy the Adventure!	212

What Next for Me? — 215

Finding Love Take #2	217
My Passions	220
Writing This Book	223
Co-Piloting 2025	225

Thanks To — 229

Foreword

Let's get something straight. This isn't just another business book.

This is a survival guide for the bold. A permission slip for the imperfect. A love letter to those who've fallen, risen, adapted, and dared to keep going when most would quit.

Nikki has written and shared something extraordinary here.

Her life.

Not because she's tried to be extraordinary but because she's been honest. And that's rarer than you think.

This book doesn't hide the cracks, it shines through them.

The grit. The guts. The graft. It's all here.

Driven to Achieve isn't theory, it's lived experience. It's lessons that have been earned, not borrowed. It's decades of real business. Real life. Real leadership.

From broken bones, a broken marriage, a broken dream that

became a nightmare, that went on to become the dream of building businesses, family and a life.

She doesn't just talk about resilience, she is resilience.

And that's why this book matters. Because too many people are fed the lie that success is shiny. Instagrammable. Perfect. It's not. It is on occasion messy. Hard. Personal.

In this book Nikki opens the door and lets you in. She shows you the chaos, the choices, the comebacks, and this is important, that most of all, the character it takes to keep going, to make your reality one you want to live.

This isn't about ego. It's about evidence. That you can and will be knocked down and yet still build something beautiful.

That leadership isn't always loud; it's in the decisions made when no one's watching.

That success isn't found in the spotlight, it's built in the shadows, in the grind, in the quiet belief that says, "I'm not done yet."

Whether you're running your own business, leading a team, or just trying to lead yourself, there is something in these pages that will hit home.

Something that'll make you sit up, take stock, and step forward.

In my career, I've met & worked with thousands of people in my time.

I met and worked with Nikki.

She's one of a kind.

Sassy, steely, smart, funny, fearless, and not afraid to show and share the scars that shaped her. So that you can look and share the ones that shaped you.

She's written this not for attention, but for impact. It delivers.

Read it. Feel it. Then do something with it.

Because this is your fuel now.

In life, there are talkers and doers.

Nikki is both.

What about you?

You absolutely will have what it takes, but do you have what it really takes? Because the lessons and teachings in the following chapters, mean you're about to find out…

Brad Burton
MotivationalLeader.co.uk

About This Book

2025 marks a momentous milestone for me: 32 eventful and exciting years in business.

Wow, that blows my mind!

It's hard to believe how far I've come, and when I stop to reflect, I realise it's time to summarise the lessons I've learned along the way and share my stories, for there are many.

I started at the tender age of 15, not having a clear career path in mind. I didn't have a specific goal of working in business, it sort-of just happened. Growing up in a family where business was always around me, I eventually found myself falling into it naturally.

It wasn't a conscious decision or a defined career choice; it was simply doing what I had always known and building on the skills and knowledge I had absorbed from a young age.

Fast forward 32 years, and I realise, almost unknowingly, I'd been completing an apprenticeship in business, my very own MBA if you will, learning the ropes, failing occasionally, but growing every single year.

With each challenge, I've built more resilience, more determination, and developed the grit that is essential to thrive in business and in life itself.

Throughout my journey, there have been incredible highs, with awards and celebrations, but also deeply painful lows, disappointments, and failures.

But you know what? I wouldn't change a thing. Every experience has shaped me into who I am today, and for that, I am deeply grateful.

This book combines stories from my own career and personal journey, anecdotes from business people I know personally and admire, and valuable lessons that have shaped my path. This is not a book that needs to be read cover to cover; just dip in and out as you wish.

What I've learned is that every journey is unique. My experiences are mine, and yours will be yours. However, I hope that in some way, you'll find something that resonates with you, something you can take away and use in your own life and business.

If nothing else, I hope you simply enjoy reading these words of mine.

So, here goes...

Photos from my career can be seen on my website:
nikkibutlin.co.uk

Who Am I?

I'm a mother, a partner, and the Finance Director of a multi-million-pound company.

I'm both introvert and extrovert.

I like my own company and that of others.

I like to sing when the feeling takes me and be quiet at times when I need to recharge.

I prefer a documentary to a book, and a colourful pie chart to a 10-page explanation of the same information.

I'm both witty and serious and can morph my character depending on the environment I find myself in.

I prefer being second in command to first.

I love a spreadsheet… I'm actually a closet geek.

I like reading numbers – they tell a story.

If it doesn't exist already, I'll try and find a way of making it happen.

I prefer not to worry about things until there's something major to worry about.

I'm generally laid back but occasionally uptight.

I've clocked up over 32 years of working with businesses, right next to the founder on almost every occasion, that's when I wasn't the founder myself.

My biggest joys have been building teams, showing them the way and then letting them get on with it, encouraging from the sidelines.

I can work people out pretty quickly and where they'll fit in a team (if at all).

I'm still a work in progress but I have plenty of wisdom and knowledge to share.

I've had major wins and catastrophic losses.

I've been broken, crying on my knees, but have risen back again through sheer grit and determination.

I'm still figuring it all out, the same as everyone else.

I know everyone is fighting their own battles… I work hard to remember that.

I like to keep life simple. Stress is not meant for long-term consumption. It's for keeping you alive in life-threatening situations.

Who am I writing for? Myself mainly, as an expression and cathartic outlet. But... if someone reads this and takes a nugget on board then that's a bonus.

Who are you?

Part 1

Building Character

Introduction

These are my stories about how my character has been built, shaping me into the person I am today. I'm starting with this topic because, in my experience, it's one of the most critical factors in determining long-term success.

Your ability to navigate challenges, adapt under pressure, and push through adversity, will define not only your career but your personal growth as well.

We are all born with a unique character. Anyone with more than one child will tell you that despite sharing the same parents, siblings can have completely different personalities.

My sister and I are a prime example of that. Born from the same parents with the same genes, but chalk and cheese otherwise.

But character isn't just something you inherit, it's something you build.

And when life throws you into choppy waters, whether in business or your personal life, that's when your character will be tested the most.

So how do you strengthen it?

The answer is simple – Step outside your comfort zone!

Growth doesn't happen in comfort.

It happens in the messy, uncertain, and unpredictable moments in life.

Want a fast track to character development?

Start a business.

(I say this with a slight smile and a chuckle, because anyone who's done it knows exactly what I mean!)

No degree, course, or textbook can truly prepare you for the reality of running a business.

Take Covid-19 as an example.

Who on earth saw that coming?

I bet that less than 1% of business plans or forecasts written in 2019 included a contingency for a global pandemic.

For me, it was one of the most challenging business episodes I've ever faced.

But we adapted. The business I worked for at the time came out the other side, and I walked away with lessons, experience and resilience that no qualification could ever have taught me.

What did I learn during that time? I thrive under pressure. I can handle and manage people in a crisis. With knowledge of the business and the right people alongside me, I become an army general, coordinating the troops. Some people freeze in difficult situations.

I find my strength. And that's what character building is all about.

You can't develop resilience overnight.

You build it by facing challenges, embracing discomfort, and proving to yourself, over and over, that you can handle whatever comes your way, until it becomes the absolute norm. Then it's so solidly embedded in your character, it's second nature when needed again.

So, start now!

Push yourself. Step outside your comfort zone.

Because when the storm hits, and it will... you'll be ready.

Childhood Initiative

Throughout writing this first part, on 'Building Character', I started to think back to my childhood and the adventures I used to get up to. It got me thinking about the old adage of nature vs. nurture. So, I want to share some stories where it's apparent that I probably had an entrepreneurial spirit from the very beginning.

It's been a fascinating and amusing section to write so I hope you enjoy it and let me know what you think... are our characters formed at birth, are they developed by our surroundings or a bit of both?

Dial 999

My dad's genius way of teaching us how to contact the emergency services was in our first house when I was around six years old. Mum was out for the evening and Dad was in charge of putting us to bed. He'd read to us for a bit and then would normally leave us to get off to sleep, with the jewellery box music singing quietly in the background. On this particular occasion he pretended to be asleep. He just laid there motionless for what seemed like a lifetime and no amount of nudging or shouting in his ear was waking him.

After around 5 minutes I decided it was best for my sister and me to go downstairs and wait up for Mum to come home. I had no idea what time it was or how long she would be, but off we went.

I think he left us for another 10 minutes, again a lifetime in the mind of a six-year-old, and eventually came downstairs to our delight and sheer relief. We hadn't killed him. Phew.

We then had an informative talk about how to dial 999 in the event of an emergency, or when your parents pretend to be stupid arses! It was a lesson remembered.

Splatz

Summer holidays were rather boring for me, and I hated Sundays because nothing was going on. This was before the time of Sunday opening hours and you had to just occupy yourself, so I did. Mum and Dad were either working at their showroom or just tired from a busy week. Our grandparents lived at the back of the house in an annex Dad had built, so we always had someone looking after us but in terms of stimulation and enjoyment my sister and I had to make it up, like many kids in the 80s. No phones, no gaming or computers.

My sister liked to read, and I liked to be outside. We had a shed in the garden that Dad didn't really use so I commandeered it for our new playhouse. My grandparents donated some old chairs and a table along with some crockery and I set about decorating it. I found some white paint, asked Dad if I could brighten up the dull brown external woodwork and then asked him to buy me some red paint, which he duly did to keep me quiet.

The shed had a side garden and a spare wall which I painted white and then the word 'Splatz' in red across it. We now had our own play area for when our friends visited, and it looked absolutely shocking! But it was ours.

Despite my interior design efforts, Splatz turned out not to be the cosiest of places, so one other boring Sunday afternoon I used some of Dad's unused scaffolding to build a tower, equipped with a stepladder up to the second floor which was laid out with floorboards in the form of an old door I had found lying around. Health and safety be damned! A few blankets over the top and we had our very own two-storey playhouse including pool, (paddling pool) which we would jump into from the top floor, much to Mum's anxiety at us hurting ourselves. It was brilliant!

It was a great summer after all, full of mud pies, dens, paddling pools and laughter. I wonder if today's generation have such opportunities to be inventive out of boredom now that they live in the digital age with constant entertainment on a phone or tablet? I think it all enhanced my creative skills and fostered an impulse to keep busy and build stuff. I am actually grateful for that boredom. I was forced to create my own amusement, so I did.

School magazine

During my first year in high school, I created my first business, even fully equipped with a team. Get me! I can't remember exactly what prompted it but from memory it may have been from watching the 80s kids' programme *Press Gang* led by the actress Julia Sawalha, who later played Saffy in *Ab Fab*. Julia played the lead character Lynda Day, editor of the school newspaper the *Junior Gazette*. I loved it. The dynamics and the stories must have inspired something in me because I went into school one day and put the idea of a magazine to my group of friends. We would sell it at our old primary school located just down the road.

I assembled the team (with me as editor of course) and off we trotted to put our proposal to our old Headmaster. Our offering was simple – we would produce the magazine full of interesting articles and quizzes and sell it for 10p, with the proceeds going to the school. Reluctantly he agreed to give it a go, I think more so to get rid of us and so we set up our first planning meeting.

Again, I can't quite remember details of the content, because it was almost 40 years ago, but I do remember using Dad's new photocopier to print off copies, and then we sat on the playground floor folding the pages and putting the finished articles together.

Off we went to proudly deliver them and set about planning the next edition.

It raised a few pounds for the school but after about three or four publications my first encounter with 'creative differences' pulled us apart. It's funny thinking back on it now, how it came together and how it fell apart. We did what we set out to do, but I imagine my people skills weren't fully developed at that time and I may have been overbearing and ever so slightly bossy… who knows? I can laugh about it now and realise that the business bug started young.

Locked out

My sister and I usually walked or cycled the two miles home from high school and, once Mum and Dad had their business showroom near King's Lynn, our grandparents would be at home to see us in. Except inconveniently for us they sometimes liked to have their own fun at the Over 60s Club and went off for day trips. How inconsiderate of them!

Anyway, the first time we found ourselves locked out we walked back half a mile to the telephone box to make a reverse charge call to Mum and Dad's office. For those too young to remember reverse call charges, if you didn't have any change to make a call from a telephone box, usually 10p for a quick call, you had to phone the operator on 100 and ask them to call the number for you and request permission to put you through.

Thankfully, Mum accepted the call and we told her of our predicament, and she drove home to let us in. At least it wasn't raining that day!

The second time it happened we couldn't be bothered to walk back to the village, so I scoured the house for any open windows and discovered the one to our parents' bedroom was slightly open. Bingo! Just the small issue of getting up there. No matter, I found an extendable stepladder in the garage and put it up against the wall, asking my sister to hold it at the bottom. I think she thought I was crazy but if it meant we didn't need to walk back to the village she was fully on board with my plan.

Up I climbed in my short school skirt, in full view of the A47 bypass of traffic that passed our house around 200 yards away. The ladder didn't quite reach fully but I managed to pull the window open, stood on the top rung (not recommended and quite dangerous) and clambered into the bedroom. Yes!

Downstairs, I let my sister in, we got our after-school drinks and biscuits and when Mum and Dad returned home, they were none the wiser!

Groovy gang

I set up my first membership club in my early teens, again out of boredom while sitting in our parents' showroom one weekend. There was my sister and a friend, and I devised the membership rules and certificate and made them both write out their forms and learn the rules. No wonder my sister didn't like playing with me most of the time – I was so bossy! I made up a secret code and we wrote letters when we were apart only to be read by each other. How blooming crazy is that?

What have I learnt writing about my childhood initiative?

Lots!

I'm bossy, I'm a born leader, I had to learn people skills, I'm good at creating things, I can usually get myself out of a pickle and I can think on my feet. I'll also never be bored because I can keep myself occupied. All great life skills that have stayed with me and grown over the years into positives, thank God!

Break A Leg (or an arm)!

Round one

If you're a fan of *Gardeners' World,* you'll know the presenter, Nick Bailey. Nick and I, along with our siblings, went to the same village school and would often be in each other's gardens during the summer. Nick was a year or so older than me, so I didn't know him all that well, but he was always tending to his part of the garden whenever I went round. It was obviously his calling in life.

It was on one of the last days of the summer holidays in 1987 and we were playing on a ramp that Nick's father had built for us to cycle over. I was stood on the flat end about to walk off it when my sister and friend stood on the top side of it, flipping me up into the air and then landing awkwardly on my arm.

I heard a noise but had no pain at the time. I remember holding my right arm up to the late afternoon sunlight and the forearm being square in half. A complete clean break across both bones. Yeah... Ouch!

I held the break to support it while running into the house. Chaos ensued and everyone was panicking.

"Let go", asked Nick's mum, to which I cried, "I can't!"

It was a traumatic time and I ended up in hospital waiting for it to be set in plaster and about to miss my cousin's wedding happening that weekend, where my sister was to be bridesmaid.

The first day back in school that September I was the talk of the classroom with my shiny new plaster cast. While others told stories of their adventurous holidays I sat back while the boys drew rude pictures on it. I did develop a new skill though out of the monstrosity of this event. I discovered I could write pretty legibly with my left hand. Who knew? I remember apologising to my teacher about not being able to write as many words as the other kids had done during the morning's task. He looked at me, rolled his eyes and chuckled. See, every challenge always throws up an opportunity somewhere.

So, September 1987, I'm ambidextrous, can't swim or do sports, which I love, and have missed a good family party.

Back for plates

Unsurprisingly, as both forearm bones had broken clean through and I'd simply been put in a plaster cast, the six-week x-ray check-up showed things were not mending well.

So, back into hospital I went, to have metal plates inserted. A full-on cut-your-arm-open-and-drill-some-metal-to-the-bones procedure type of thing! My second general anaesthetic at the age of 10.

That hurt!

And to make matters worse, when they were strapping me back up in plaster, they strapped the cotton wool too tight around my wrist, so my hand swelled up to the size of a balloon. They weren't going to discharge me without the swelling going down, so I visited this lovely lady down in the plastering department who took what looked like a mini chainsaw to my arm. I thought she was going to cut right through me so I screamed out. She told me to be quiet.

Distraught, in pain and bandaged up, I returned home in the hope that this time it had worked. Luckily, it had, but I now had two tramline scars which I still have to this day. These make for a good conversation starter during the summer months when people ask me, "What did you do to your arm?"

"Well, I was 10 years old…"

Breaking my arm – round two

The following February I had returned to gymnastics. I was a good gymnast, although could never do a back flip. I was strong for my age, with good core muscles, and the bars were my favourite.

It was during one evening's practice whilst doing my thing on the asymmetric bars that the coach decided to take the big crash mat away, leaving a three-inch deep thing like one of those sleeping mattresses for camping, as I'd been doing my routine so well up to that point.

As you may have guessed, that night I wasn't as good as I'd previously been and fell to the ground having missed the top bar and fell on my hands to break my fall.

Another snap, some pain and a quick trip to A&E showed that I had broken my wrist due to the strength from the rest of the arm with the added reinforcement of the plates. Jeez, can you make this stuff up?

Back in plaster, back watching from the sidelines during swimming lessons and back writing left-handed.

Removal of plates

The following summer of 1988, in between primary and high school, I returned to hospital for the final time (with this incident anyway) and had the plates removed. As I was still young it was important for my bones to keep growing naturally and the metal would have prevented that from happening.

I kept them in a bag for a few years and would bring them out each Halloween. They must have been thrown out at some point because they're nowhere to be found now. Probably a good thing.

I can still feel the bump along the outer bone in my arm and my pretty funky scars to prove I'm not making any of this up. I may get arthritis later on, but I've done quite well to stay out of plaster since that episode.

Bailing Out of Sixth Form

I've never been an academic, but I worked hard in my last two years of high school and did well in my exams. That success led my well-meaning teachers to steer me towards sixth form and university. Looking back, I don't ever remember being shown any real alternatives.

However, as a true future entrepreneur, I wanted to carve my own path.

At the time, my parents had been running their double-glazing business for about six years. That summer I had worked in their office, answering phones, handling admin and assisting the surveyor in processing the UPVC orders. In my first week there, I asked if I could reorganise his office because the trays weren't aligned with the workflow. He gave me the green light, and I set about restructuring the space. I've always had a logical brain for processes and systems, and by rearranging the desks and placing the trays in order of job progression it massively improved the systems and he complimented me on my initiative.

That summer was busy, and I loved it. Having my own money was a great feeling; I no longer had to ask Mum and Dad for pocket money to go shopping. Aside from the occasional clothing or toiletry purchase, I didn't need much.

Then sixth form started. It was a brand-new school for me, and it felt like the students who were already there had received a completely different education and GCSE preparation than those of us coming from my high school. My peers and I felt like fish out of water. The entire process was intimidating.

Still, as the diligent student I was, I entered my economics, history, and geography classes with enthusiasm. And... I was completely and utterly bored.

By the October half-term, as I stared at my homework on Hitler, I found myself wondering, where was all this going to take me? Now, I love learning about World War II and have gained far more knowledge over the years through sheer curiosity about the subject. But at that particular moment, I just wanted out.

I didn't know exactly what I wanted to do, but I knew that sixth form wasn't it. I asked Dad if I could join the family business full-time. It took him all of two seconds to say yes. Understandably, Mum was apprehensive, worried about my future and concerned that I was giving up too soon.

But I knew my own mind.

My old teachers and sixth form tutors told me I was making a mistake. They warned me it would be much harder to go back later. I could see the disappointment in their faces. But something inside me screamed that I was doing the right thing.

So I left. I went to work, I earned money, and I built up some savings. Then, a year later, when I realised that understanding finance would be beneficial for the family business, I took myself off to night school to study bookkeeping.

To this day, I do not for one second regret the decision to quit school. I have no regrets about not going to university. That route simply wasn't for me.

I learn best by doing, by hands-on experience, by being shown.

My instincts were shouting at me and, luckily, I listened to them.

Finding Love Take #1

I met Steve in a nightclub in King's Lynn – you remember the kind, with the sticky floors, right?

It was the mid-90s, Britpop was a thing and schnapps and lemonade was my drink of the day (or night to be more precise). A guy called Carl who worked for my parents was one of Steve's oldest friends, along with another guy called Simon, so we started hanging around together, the three guys along with me and my school friend Katy.

A few months passed and Steve and I started seeing each other, quickly becoming inseparable and after a mere six months we bought a house together. What? Ha, you could do that back then at that age! It was a pretty bold move for a 19- and 24-year-old at that time, with lots of people telling us we were rushing into things and "Who wants a mortgage round their necks that young?!" Our thinking was that if a mortgage was for 25 years wouldn't it be better to get going now and have it paid off sooner? Plus, if things didn't work out, we would simply split the sale proceeds and go our separate ways. Happy Days!

We loved putting our home together and after a year Steve joined the family firm in a sales role, which he was great at, a real people person and easy to get along with. He'd lost his mum aged eight to pneumonia and his father had raised him and his older brother alone. My family really loved him, and we would spend endless Sunday dinners and evenings together socialising as well as all working together.

I remember us being really happy in those early days – we had our home, our careers, we took great holidays and life was great.

He proposed on my 21st birthday in the Lake District and we married the following year in the village church, followed by a marquee reception in my parents' front garden. It was a fabulous day. All the planning and preparation came together, and it was so lovely to have our family and friends around us. We jetted off on the Sunday for two weeks in the Maldives. A blissful time.

Singing

My character is multi-faceted, and my CV is eclectic, to say the least. Everything I've done, however, has given me a skill that I use in business today. I used to be a singer, firstly as a solo performer, singing to backing tracks in social clubs and pubs in my early 20s, and later as part of a band in my mid-30s.

I did it first and foremost because I loved to sing, but as I've grown older, I've realised it provided me with a skill I still use today. I can confidently stand on a stage and present to people.

Over the years, I've given numerous talks and presentations, and the skills I have in my toolbox for preparation, rehearsal and execution have stood me in good stead. I know exactly what to do, how to prepare for the audience listening, and have honed my performance over time.

There is something grounding about having my feet planted firmly on stage, microphone in hand, delivering a song, a talk or a presentation. Strange, isn't it? Because you'd expect it to be a time for nerves and stumbling over words. But for me, it's exhilarating. The rush, especially once I've found my flow after a few minutes, is rather addictive, I must admit.

I never did anything related to singing at school, I was too shy. It wasn't until I left school that the bug bit me. As a 15-year-old, I would practice at home alone, losing track of time, singing along to my favourite songs for hours.

First time out in public

My first public performance was during a family holiday to Spain. The hotel was holding a competition, and Dad urged me to enter, knowing how much I loved to sing. Still shy, but eager to perform, I went for it. After my first song, I walked back to our table along the outer walkway and took my seat. Dad congratulated me and then suggested that, after my next song, I walk straight down the middle of the crowd. He said something along the lines of, "Walk back like a star".

I won the competition that night, received a bottle of bubbly, and we celebrated for the rest of the holiday.

Going professional

When I started singing professionally and getting paid at 20, I was really nervous. But I wanted to face my fears and stand up in front of a crowd. In the early years, I avoided eye contact, as I was too scared to see people's reactions. I would simply sing my song, hope they liked it, and promptly exit stage left. The part I found uncomfortable was speaking to people afterwards. They were usually complimentary, but I felt awkward acknowledging praise. Odd, isn't it? One for the psychologists!

Over time, as I built a reputation, I was invited to sing at Masonic

Balls, Golf Clubs on New Year's Eve, charity events, Burns Night celebrations, and weddings. Dad would come along with as many people as he could pin down. I had my own groupies! It was hard work but fun. I had a full-time job, so the weeks were packed, with Sundays usually the only rest day, spent doing nothing but watching TV.

One August bank holiday, I took on three back-to-back nights. Ouch! That was gruelling. I remember slumping into the bath on the Monday night, completely shattered. Starting out, I was charging £80 for a pub gig, which was the going rate at the time. By the time I 'retired' at 24 (for the first time), I was commanding £300 for prestigious events.

Talent competitions

I used to spend hours rehearsing alone at my parents' house, where I kept my equipment. My competitive nature pushed me to enter talent competitions, one of which was held at the Princess Theatre in Hunstanton in the summer of 2000. First prize was a solo show at the theatre, right up my street now my confidence had increased! I made it through the first and second heats and landed a place in the final. Mum and Dad bought me a beautiful, sparkly Frank Usher dress, and I treated myself to new heels. (What is it about heels that makes you feel fabulous?)

The night of the final, I belted out my songs with all my might to a packed theatre. I couldn't have done more, but first place wasn't meant to be that time. A close second to a local guy, respectable, but it lit a fire in my belly. I wanted my own show in a theatre. Speaking with Dad (my No. 1 fan) afterwards, we were both disappointed at the result. But in true entrepreneurial style, we came up with the idea of hiring the Corn Exchange in King's Lynn and putting on our own show.

Headlining

So that's what we did. We booked a director we'd met at another competition, hired dancers from a Cambridge studio, and I brought in a guest male singer for a duet.

I crunched the numbers (on a spreadsheet of course) and figured we could actually make a profit from ticket sales, until Dad, ever the strategist, suggested we get the show filmed. That way, I'd have a show reel to market myself for future bookings. He was building my marketing assets before I even knew what that meant!

The show took place on a Tuesday evening in late March 2001. We gave away a lot of tickets to fill the audience – sometimes, you have to do that to gain traction. If you do a great job, people will refer and recommend you, which creates momentum. The evening was a success. The feedback was overwhelmingly positive and unbeknown to me, a few journalists were in the audience. Their published reviews were glowing.

My clock was ticking

The bookings kept coming, my fees kept increasing, and my diary was full for the rest of the year. But something else was calling me – I could hear my biological clock ticking at 24 (a little early nowadays I guess but I've always been ahead of the game). I didn't want to be an older mum, and with such a full schedule, I knew I had to plan ahead. Pregnancy and gigging weren't going to mix well.

Pregnancy #1

So, I set my retirement date for the end of 2001, going out with a literal bang on New Year's Eve. I became pregnant quickly in 2002, and in typical style, we decided to move house before the baby was due. But this little one wasn't meant for this world.

A week before our move, at 11 weeks pregnant, I started losing blood. It was confirmed at the hospital the day before our move, we had lost the baby. The whole family was devastated. In true Nikki fashion, though, I kept going, packing the removal van the next morning. It wasn't until the following weekend, after being admitted to hospital in tremendous pain and losing a lot of blood, that the grief started to hit me.

A couple of months later it hadn't passed, and I found myself on the floor, crying uncontrollably, ending up depressed at my 'failure'. I was so used to setting goals and achieving them that I didn't deal with failure well. Mother Nature has different plans though sometimes.

A full eight months followed of 'trying' my hardest to get pregnant again. I was so stressed, looking back now, there was no way it was going to happen while I was in that state. By the time Christmas came I was exhausted and needed to stop planning everything in my life and just have some fun. We decided that we'd enjoy Christmas and if I wasn't pregnant in the new year we would book a holiday to Florida.

Pregnancy #2

It's funny how the mind works. Once I relaxed, took the pressure off and started focusing on other things, it happened. Nine months after losing the first baby, I fell pregnant again. This time, the sickness was immediate and relentless, and I knew it meant this baby was strong. I was right. In September 2003, our little girl arrived, ready to shake up our world!

Motherhood

Holy mother of Mary, Jesus, and all the orphans! Where do I even begin with this one?

When it comes to shaping my character, this experience is a biggie – without a doubt, the hardest job I've ever done.

Being a mother

We were blessed with a spirited, determined, and fiercely independent child who is now out in the world, smashing life. She's inherited grit, quick wit, and a refusal to settle for an ordinary existence, traits that come from both sides of her gene pool.

I'm beyond proud of the woman she is becoming. She's bright, sharp, and has the gift of the gab, climbing her own career ladder with confidence. Watching her thrive is a joy and a privilege.

But let's not sugarcoat it.

Raising a spirited, gifted child is an absolute, relentless, and sometimes soul-crushing, nightmare! I know she will be laughing reading this because we've had numerous hysterical chats over the years about her early life and character.

I chuckle as I write this because, oh boy, have we been on a roller coaster together.

The early years – From angel to chaos in six weeks

For the first six weeks, we were those parents, you know, the ones who smugly breeze through baby groups, boasting about their perfect child. We had it all – peaceful nights, no fuss, life was complete.

And then, on the day she turned six weeks old, the universe said, "Haha, just kidding!"

First came the colic. Every evening, we endured hours of crying, desperately trying to soothe her discomfort. Nothing worked except driving her around the block until she passed out from exhaustion. The military-level operation of removing her from the car, carrying her upstairs, and placing her in the cot without waking her became our nightly ritual.

As if colic wasn't enough, eczema followed – full body, red, itchy, and relentless.

Her once soft baby skin was red raw and sore. We tried every cream, lotion and potion the doctor prescribed. Our bathroom cabinets overflowed, but nothing worked.

Desperate for answers – The allergy breakthrough

By the time she was nine months old, about to start nursery, we were at our wits' end. One day, wandering through town, I spotted a Dr. China shop advertising allergy testing.

Could they even test a baby? Was it a scam?

I didn't care. At that point, I would have paid anything to get to the bottom of this.

They took a tiny sample of her hair and sent it off. £40 later, I had a detailed report listing every food, detergent and medicine she had an allergy or intolerance to.

Sitting in the car, staring at pages of highlighted items, I felt overwhelmed. How was I supposed to manage this?

But, after digesting the results, it boiled down to two main culprits: dairy and wheat.

We immediately switched her to dairy-free and wheat-free alternatives (which, let's be honest, smelled revolting), and within two weeks, her eczema was almost gone.

Bingo. We had cracked it!

Battling the nursery to keep her in

Just when I thought we had turned a corner, I got called into the nursery. She was now nine months old and was now attending the local Montessori nursery school.

They were threatening to expel her. I hadn't quite envisaged being dragged into the headteacher's office when my child was at such an early age but hey, motherhood was turning out to be nothing like I had planned it.

Why was I called? Because nuts had also been flagged on her allergy list, and they feared she might go into anaphylactic shock and die.

I had to fight tooth and nail to convince them that the worst-case scenario was a flare-up of eczema, not a life-threatening reaction.

An hour-long battle later, they relented. She stayed. Phew!

Baby crisis number one... sorted!

The toddler years – Stubbornness, genius, and sleepless nights

At two years old, she fought bedtime like a seasoned warrior.

I remember looking at her, staring me down with the willpower of a horse, wondering how on earth a toddler could match my determination so perfectly.

At the same age, she was given a shape-sorting book, one of those where you take out the pieces and put them back.

She got every single shape right, first time, every time.

Our jaws hit the floor.

Between colic, eczema and relentless bedtime battles, I often asked myself:

"Where is the peaceful baby I ordered?"

"Where is my Mother Earth instinct that I swear I selected at checkout?"

Nowhere to be frickin' seen!

The school years – A star student, a messy bedroom, and the battles at home

In school, she was a star pupil.

Never in trouble, always well-mannered. Out in public, she was an angel.

But at home? Different story.

Her bedroom looked like a war zone. The mess got worse as she got older. Eventually, she just told me not to go in if it bothered me so much.

I had to respect the logic, even if I hated the mess.

Motherhood – The hardest and most rewarding challenge of my life

Would I change a thing?

Not for a second.

Being her mum has challenged me, shaped me, and made me stronger.

She's now a young woman fully prepared for the first stage of adulthood, with skills, confidence and resilience that will stay with her long after I'm gone.

Stepping into a new role – Bonus mum

Life has a funny way of giving us unexpected gifts.

Now, I have the privilege of being honorary step-mum to my partner's daughter, a truly lovely, kind and warm young lady who too has determination and is forging her way headlong into adulthood.

I was so nervous the first time we met, hoping she'd like me. But when she walked in, she came straight over and gave me a great big hug. We've been friends ever since, which I just love. Both she and my daughter get along wonderfully and as they were both pretty much adults when we got together it's been slightly easier than becoming a step-parent to young children.

My role as step-mum? Support in the background, be there if and when she needs me, and have her back for the rest of my life. Because family isn't just about blood, it's about love, support, and showing up.

Mother Earth (I think not!)

Motherhood has been a challenge, a lesson, and an honour.

I've made mistakes, cried in frustration, and questioned everything. But I've also taught, guided, and loved fiercely, and will do so for the rest of my life.

And that?

That is my one of my greatest achievements.

Hypnotherapy

My first encounter with hypnotherapy came when my daughter was just nine months old. Struggling with motherhood, I knew I needed help.

I was hesitant at first, this "new-fangled" thing seemed a bit out there, and I'll admit, I was slightly apprehensive that I might walk out of the session making chicken noises! But any fears I had quickly disappeared when I met the wonderful woman who would guide me through it.

From the start, we clicked. She explained hypnosis in a way that made sense, breaking down the myths and misconceptions and putting me completely at ease. At the end of our first session, she led me through a guided relaxation and handed me a CD, instructing me to listen to it every night before bed. So, I did. A few weeks and a handful of sessions later, I started to notice a shift.

I felt more confident. The little things that used to bug me no longer did. My mindset had shifted in a way I hadn't expected. It dawned on me that this transformation must have come from the positive affirmations on that CD, words sinking in just before sleep, gently rewiring my thoughts. I found it all so fascinating and beneficial that I wanted to learn more.

Training

Determined to understand the practice on a deeper level, I enrolled at the Essex Institute of Clinical Hypnosis in Southend in 2006. For a year, I attended monthly weekend training sessions, joining a group of around 25 students, many of whom became good friends.

Our lead tutor was Terence Watts, an incredible teacher and the author of *Warrior, Settler and Nomad*, a brilliant book on personality types. The course was intense and immersive, covering everything from basic hypnosis techniques to psychosis, trauma, stress, anxiety, grief, smoking cessation, and weight loss. We were warned that some of the content could be triggering, and therapists were on hand for anyone who needed support. That level of care only deepened my respect for the profession. I was hooked.

As the course neared its end, we were encouraged to start preparing to practice professionally. True to form, I jumped in headfirst. I built a website, printed business cards, set up a home therapy room, and ran some small ads in local village newsletters. Before long, clients started booking in. I'll admit, I was nervous – what if I couldn't bring someone back out of hypnosis? (For the record, that doesn't happen. All hypnosis is self-hypnosis. If you don't want to go under, you won't. You're always in control!)

At the end of my training, I earned my Diploma in Hypnotherapy and Psychotherapy and was honoured to be voted by my peers as the "Student Most Likely to Succeed". That recognition led to a nomination for Student of the Year, where I was invited back to Southend for an interview with a judging panel.

I spoke passionately about my work, particularly my experience with hypno-analysis, a deep free-association technique for uncovering the root causes of long-standing issues. I explained how I could visualise what my clients were experiencing, intuitively guiding them to the next step. That passion must have come through because I was awarded Overall Student of the Year at the annual EICH gathering in 2007.

Frog Lady

One of my favourite and most memorable clients was a lady who called, detailing what I thought was her "fear of dogs". When she arrived at the consulting room and we began speaking, it transpired that she actually had a fear of frogs, not dogs. Interesting, I thought. During the first couple of sessions, she relayed to me both in and out of hypnosis about how when she was younger she'd been playing in her cousin's garden and on one occasion a frog jumped across her path, frightening her. When she ran into the house wanting her mum, crying and afraid, she wasn't there and her aunt had to console her.

Around week 3 or 4 she came back in and I always did the "So, how has your week been?" catch up. To which she immediately replied, "It's not about the frogs, is it? It's about my mum!" I smiled knowingly and said, "Do you think so?" To which we both laughed.

What had happened during the sessions is that an event from her past had been summoned up into her adult conscious mind and she had worked out that the emotion was in fact connected with feeling alone and scared about her mum not being present. The fear had been connected to the frog as a child by association. Another session later and she relayed that she was never going to want to hug a frog but that she felt a lot better and was no longer frightened of them. I agreed that I would not want to hug one either! I then went on to help her with her fear of lifts but that's another story.

Two happy years of practice

For two years, I ran a successful hypnotherapy practice, working with clients on a wide range of issues. One of the biggest lessons I learned was that the problem a client initially presents with is rarely the real issue, it's just the symptom. The real work is in uncovering the cause. But as much as I loved the work, I eventually realised that lone working wasn't for me. I thrive in team environments, and hypnotherapy isn't scalable unless you run a training school, which I had no interest in doing. So, I reluctantly closed my practice and moved on to new challenges.

That being said, I use my psychotherapy training every single day. Understanding how people tick, different personality types, and the fact that there's always something deeper going on, has been invaluable in business.

Skills I use today

Now, as the Head of Internal HR at ASC Metals, my ability to read people, handle complex team dynamics, and approach situations with empathy, has made all the difference. At the end of the day, we're all human, and if there's one thing hypnotherapy has taught me, it's the power of compassion, understanding, and truly listening to others.

Franchising

Our cleaning company

My first knowledge of franchising came when Steve and I set up Blue Sky Cleaning in January 2006. Aimed as an added value service to the double-glazing company my parents owned, we thought there might be 'legs' in our idea.

The beautiful constructions my parents and their team were building onto the back of people's homes would, in around a year or two's time, need cleaning. The customers were often of an age where physical mobility was limited and on research there didn't appear to be anyone offering a specialised service, particularly the one that we had in mind. There were plenty of window cleaners around but no one offering conservatory cleaning.

Aha! A new business venture beckoned…

On one of our first planning meetings at a Wetherspoons pub in King's Lynn (it's always good to brainstorm new ideas in the pub, I've found), Steve said it would have the possibility of being franchised in the future if we got the initial business model correct.

I'd heard of the term franchising before but knew very little about it. So off I went with my research notebook, as well as making a to-do list for setting up our new business. At this stage all we had was an idea and my list of what we needed to do to get started, but after reading up on exactly what franchising was, I could see its potential. From the outset we planned everything around the business eventually being scaled into a national operation, and that started with the name.

If you're going to scale up a business and in particular franchise it, you need to create a 'business in a box'. Everything from trademarking the name, to the vehicle signage, to the operation methods, to the way you found your customers, must be a model able to be replicated.

We named the business 'Blue Sky Cleaning' and within a month we had a very irate man on the phone who was complaining that we were 'passing off' on his trade name. They were a completely different business, and we battled our case. He didn't have a leg to stand on, but it was rather unnerving nonetheless.

Anyway, we eventually changed the name to 'Cleanservatory' which seemed more brand-able and did what it said on the tin in terms of telling people what we were about.

We built the business up between 2006 and 2011, with Steve working long hours, attending trade shows, and managing our team of 3 cleaners and vans. We were turning over in excess of £10,000 a month and had built a solid customer base in our area. Customers were on at least an annual repeating service, if not more frequently, and Steve had discovered a product that could be put on conservatory roofs that would effectively 'seal' out the mould build-up for 12 months in between cleans.

It was time to franchise and set up our pilot operation.

Now, with anything in business, when you're scaling up, investment is involved. We were now setting up a new franchising company as a separate entity and looking for funding from a bank to help us develop the business essentials. From memory it was going to cost around £25,000 to complete this stage. A lot of money. We did discuss whether to stay as we were, as our basic business was generating a good income, but we went back to our initial conversation and plans from the outset. It could be scaled, and we *were* going to do it.

I left my job at the family double-glazing company to work full-time in the business and get the franchise up and running. I travelled to London to attend seminars and meet with specialist bank departments who were loaning to start-up ventures, which we were at that point.

I secured the necessary business loan, we had started writing the operation manuals, and hubby had been working on the brand bible. It was hard work again, getting another new venture off the ground but that's what it takes, and we went at it wholeheartedly.

Then in the autumn of 2011 we split up.

Yeah… didn't see that one coming, did you? Not sure I saw it coming either, which is all I intend to say about this difficult time.

Steve took the business on himself and later sold it.

In terms of knowledge and skills though… our buckets were full (no pun intended!).

Cloud Bookkeeping

After we separated and went our different ways, six months later I joined Cloud Bookkeeping, having met its founder Mandy during my franchise research period. Mandy had a great brand, a highly infectious character, and already had around 10 franchisees in her bookkeeping network. She had reached the stage where she could no longer cope with the recruiting, training and support of the growing network.

After a couple of catch-up discussions, she asked me to join Cloud Bookkeeping as her Business Development Director. Coupled with my new knowledge of the franchise industry and my business and accounting experience I helped her build the company further.

With Cloud Bookkeeping based in Harrow, I would travel down from King's Lynn to King's Cross 2–3 times a month, which was perfect for collecting my daughter from school when I was home based. Mum and Dad would look after her when I was travelling which was a huge help.

I attended trade shows and recruited new franchisees, which was great fun; talking to new people, passionate about what Mandy had to offer them and losing my voice by the end of the day.

I helped support the new recruits during their set-up phase and attended networking events to help them grow their clients and business. It was a hugely enjoyable time, and I was thriving in my role.

I found the franchising world fascinating. Full of entrepreneurs building their networks and people wanting to have their own business via a franchise model that someone else had designed. Brilliant!

What I learnt though was that not everyone is cut out to be a business owner. Some people we took on had retired young from the civil service or the forces. Some were trained accountants who had never done any actual bookkeeping. When it's a hands-on franchise and not a management model (like McDonalds for example where you place a team in) you are required to do all the tasks yourself until you grow enough to employ someone.

So, the franchisees were doing their networking to find customers on top of the actual bookkeeping work, as well as their own bookkeeping for their business. It's a tough call for someone who's never run a business before, but that's what you pay your management service fee for, the support from head office.

During my time with Cloud Bookkeeping, we entered and won the Best Growing Franchise award in 2012 and 2013. It was a brilliant time, with plenty of travel, adventure and new skills added to my toolkit!

diddi dance

My other experience with franchising was with the fabulous and equally energetic Anne-Marie Martin of diddi dance. (Yes, they are lower case d's, that's her branding!)

Anne-Marie is an ex-dancer and set up her pre-school children's dance franchise in 2005.

I met Anne-Marie at a franchise awards ceremony with Mandy and when I set up Athena Business Services in 2014 (more about this later) she contacted me for some support with her finances. I worked with diddi dance and many of its franchisees up until I sold Athena in 2019. I spoke at some of their annual conferences and Anne-Marie and her network were a joy to work with.

The franchise is still going strong, and they have a simple business model which just works and can be replicated right across the country, with Anne-Marie at the helm. A marvellous success story which I absolutely love!

Sink or Swim

Have you ever faced a situation where disaster, destruction and catastrophic failure were staring you in the face?

Yeah?

Me too.

It was at the end of 2011 as my marriage tragically broke down.

The year prior to this I had experienced a massive breakdown, one that I would not wish on anyone. It took a few months and medication to get back on my feet, with support from my family around me. Now, almost a year later, I hit absolute rock bottom again, a moment where the walls were closing in, options were running out, and I had no idea how I was going to climb out of it.

I remember standing there, a few days after knowing that my marriage was over, completely overwhelmed, in the depths of disbelief and despair, saying to myself:

"I have two choices: I can either sink or swim."

And just like that, with only two options on the table, the decision was easy.

I wasn't built to sink.

So I swam.

Choosing to fight back was one thing.

Actually doing it? That was the real challenge. I had made the decision though, that was the important thing. Getting my mindset right.

I did it. And I did it with gusto, the kind fuelled by grit, determination and sheer force of will.

That moment of adversity, pressure and sheer survival instinct became the making of me.

When you're forced to find your own solutions, push through fear and protect those who rely on you, without worrying about outside opinions, you discover exactly what you're made of.

Because it's in those breaking-point moments that we uncover our resilience, strength, and ability to fight back.

And if you ever find yourself in that position?

Remember this – You are not built to sink.

So, swim!

Part 2

Set Up, Grow & Scale

Introduction

Businesses go through multiple stages, and I've been involved with them all at the various different times.

Like raising a child, each stage has it challenges, rewards and teachings.

Here in Part 2, I would like to share some of those experiences with you.

The Family Firm

My dad, the visionary

My late dad always had a plan.

It didn't matter whether it was the house, the garden, or a business, he knew exactly what it was going to look like and how he was going to make it happen. It wasn't a vague idea or a pipe dream. It was detailed, mapped out, and most importantly, credible.

If, on the rare occasion, he didn't have the answer himself, he knew exactly who to ask. He never pretended to know it all, but he just knew how to find the right people, ask the right questions, and take action faster than most. All key entrepreneurial traits.

More than just having a plan though, he had something far more powerful – unshakeable confidence. It filled everyone around him with belief. When he spoke about his vision, whether it was building a new factory, converting a house, or creating a conservatory display, you just knew it was going to happen. That kind of certainty is a rare gift. It's what makes people follow you without hesitation. It's what makes leaders. And my dad? He was a leader in every sense of the word.

He didn't do it alone, though. Behind the vision was someone just as vital, my mum. She was there through every decision, every leap of faith, and every long day. She kept the house going, the books balanced, and the Sunday lunches a regular occurrence.

It wasn't until Dad passed away in the autumn of 2022 that we truly realised just how much she had contributed to his success. She wasn't just supporting him; she was a part of the recipe that made it all possible. Behind every visionary, there's someone quietly holding the pieces together, and that was my mum. My sister and I are forever grateful to them both.

A salesman with substance

Dad was a natural salesman. Charismatic, straight-talking, and full of conviction. But more importantly, he cared about his customers and what he was selling.

His work ethic had been forged early. Growing up on a farm in Kent, one of his first jobs was plucking chickens at the age of 13. When I traced my family tree in the early 2000s, I discovered my paternal heritage was a long line of farmers from East Sussex. This probably explains Dad's love of the outdoors and gardening right throughout his life.

Over the years, he worked in a hotel in London learning how to make his famous Marie Rose sauce, then travelled the Southeast selling greeting cards. He eventually found his feet in picture framing, with his brother Albert. Never one to be afraid of hard graft he certainly wasn't someone who waited for opportunities, he would always chase them down.

In the early 1970s, he and Mum made a fresh start in Norfolk. After working a few more years picture framing he was ready for a change. Narrowing his options down to two industries: insurance or double glazing. He picked double glazing because it was real. You could see it, touch it, stand back and admire it once the job was done. That decision would go on to shape our entire family's future.

He started out working for the big boys of the industry, Anglian and Zenith, then moved to a smaller independent company in King's Lynn called Lynn Frame to further his hands-on experience.

I seem to remember that he became disenchanted by his boss and the sheer fact he was working for someone else and not in charge of his own future. That's when Economy Windows officially began.

The first spark

I can still picture the exact moment Economy Windows was born, in August 1987. It was late summer, golden evening light streaming through the kitchen windows and Dad was sat at the kitchen table with a biro in hand, sketching something on a piece of paper. I was probably fresh in from charging around the fields behind our farmhouse with my sister and our friends, making the most of the long school holidays.

Curiosity got the better of me. I peered over his shoulder and asked what he was doing. Without looking up, he simply said, "Designing the company logo". And there it was, the first version of Economy Windows: a rough sketch of a lead-light window with the name scrawled across it in Dad's unmistakable handwriting. That biro logo may have looked simple but it represented something much bigger, the beginning of a new chapter, and a whole new family routine.

The dining room quickly became the office. The garage was rejigged as a makeshift warehouse and the kitchen was transformed into the morning meeting hub for the fitters before they went out on jobs. Life changed. My sister and I had to adapt quickly. Gone were the days of wandering down to breakfast in our PJs. Now, we had to be dressed and ready.

We were trained to answer the phone properly, take down accurate messages, and treat it all with the seriousness of a proper business. Looking back, it was our first taste of customer service and business etiquette and we loved it.

From kitchen table to thriving company

Within a year, Dad had moved the business out of the house and into its own premises in a village just outside King's Lynn. It sat right on the A47, the main route in and out of town, and it was a brilliant choice. It was highly visible, with on-site parking, and was pretty much a blank canvas.

He immediately got to work, refurbishing the warehouse, building an office at the front, and constructing full-scale conservatory models so customers could walk through the products before they made a decision.

It was classic Dad. Don't just tell people, show them. Let them feel what they're investing in. Then he went against everything he had learnt from the industry big-wigs. No deposit (what??), pay on completion (really??), no hard sell (are you crazy??) and no discounts (now you are joking!). His first price would be his best price, he would tell people.

He quickly started gaining a reputation for being the local trusted salesman. What he said is what he did, and you didn't pay a penny until you were happy with the finished job. This was a one-man crusade to make the cliché of pushy, dodgy double-glazing salespeople a thing of the past! And customers loved it!

Manufacturing

I remember going with him to look at a new factory he'd acquired, in the next village. It was just a big, empty space to me. But to him? It was already a fully operational factory. He walked me through each area, pointing out where every piece of machinery would go, where the team would work, how everything would flow. It already existed in his head. All he needed was time to bring it to life. And he did.

By 2000, Economy Windows had expanded again, now with an additional showroom in Wisbech, and a reputation as the largest double-glazing operation in the region. For a while, the business manufactured its own windows and doors, before Dad calculated it would be cheaper and more efficient to buy the products in again.

Marketing without the internet

The growth was all happening long before the internet and social media channels. Marketing back then meant full-page spreads in local papers, carefully worded flyers, and a very well-thumbed copy of *Yellow Pages*.

Later, Dad jumped on the opportunity to advertise with the newly launched KLFM Radio. I'll be honest, that one was a bit mortifying as a teenager. I'd get on the bus to sixth form and hear the jingle blasting out of the radio, followed by everyone singing it loudly just to wind me up. But it worked and people remembered the name.

Behind the scenes

While Dad was the face of the business, Mum was looking after the admin and accounts after he'd taught her the ropes. Together, they worked so well as a team. In those first couple of years, they were working seven days a week, juggling fitting teams, customers, suppliers, and everything in between. Before long a sales team were working alternate weekends, enabling Mum and Dad to take a breather and enjoy some family time.

By then, my sister and I had grown more independent, and our maternal grandparents lived with us, helping with childcare and keeping the biscuit tin full.

When I joined the family firm full-time aged 16, I brought my computer skills with me, creating pie charts for the sales team each month.

When I discovered Microsoft Access, I built a CRM to look after the current orders. I also computerised the job card system, enabling the team to look up previous contracts on the PC instead of trawling through the cabinets.

Later, I sourced a software called Adminbase to take the order planning and scheduling from clipboards to a colour-coded calendar on the computer. This was a game-changer and made us all more efficient.

I even wrote an entire office manual before heading off on a long holiday, to keep things running in my absence. It appears IT and systems were a thing for me from the start of my career.

The numbers behind the name

For over 30 years, Economy Windows served more than **30,000 customers** across Norfolk and Cambridgeshire and at its peak, the business employed 30 staff. There's something in that number obviously!

Legacy in every brick

My dad wasn't just a businessman, he was a visionary. He didn't just dream. He acted. He didn't just plan. He built. From that biro sketch at the kitchen table to creating the biggest window company in the area, he proved that with vision, courage and relentless commitment, you can create something remarkable from nothing.

He saw potential where others saw problems. He acted where

others hesitated. He turned empty buildings into production lines and rough gardens into beautiful retreats. He wasn't afraid of hard work; he thrived on it. That was his gift. That is his legacy.

My family and I are eternally grateful for him and all he did for us.

Gifts 4U UK

In 2004 the world wide web revolution was still quite a new thing. To me it was blooming genius and opened up a world full of possibilities and opportunities for the whole planet. I absolutely loved it.

The inventor, a British man called Tim Berners-Lee, gave it to the world for free! How amazing is that and how grateful we should be for this selfless act. He could have made a fricking fortune, but his values made that impossible for him. Hats off Sir Tim, we applaud you!

Our daughter was in the first year of her little life and my Earth Mother gene (I say that slightly in jest cos I'm not sure I actually have one) was fighting against my Business Bad Ass Mum gene, the one that wants to create, to sell, to earn and provide.

I discovered eBay from my hairdresser at the time. She was telling me one hair-foiled day about the new bag she'd purchased second-hand from the site. While grilling her for more information she divulged that you bid on the item, hopefully win it, send the money to a complete stranger and then (in my assessment of the whole thing) pray that they send you the item.

I was sceptical of course as my nature dictates, but once home and freshly connected via my noisy internet connection I took a look. Hmmm… so you can sell your unwanted items to people anywhere in the country (or world as it transpired) for a price, they will pay the postage and eBay will take a small commission. Ok, let's give this a go.

I scoured the house for said unwanted items and quickly found some prime targets. This was at a time before smartphones (I can't even believe that as I'm typing, it sounds ludicrous) so out came the digital camera. I took the photos, hooked the device up to the PC via a cable, downloaded the images (which took an age by the way, so I made a cuppa) and began setting up the item sale page. By the end of the auction period, I had sold the wares, beautifully packaged them up and was trotting off to the village post office, with our daughter in her pushchair.

So, as you can imagine, if you've grasped my character by now, I was firmly onto a new venture. I began hunting through the house with greater effort, finding those things we didn't use anymore – old games, ornaments, pictures, small bits of furniture, and got them listed.

Having run out of current household items I needed more! My family worried about anything not being nailed down to the floor still being there the next time they visited. I tried my best to reassure them all I wouldn't sell the car. Anyway, I decided, having learnt the system, that I could possibly go out and source products on a wholesale basis to sell.

I discovered the Spring Fair at the NEC in Birmingham, where apparently there would be halls and halls of potential items for me to sell online via my new eBay store. And so 'Gifts 4U UK' was born. My new internet online selling platform that I could run from home whilst looking after our new daughter... ah bliss!

If you've ever attended a major exhibition at the NEC, you'll know it's absolutely massive and many of the shows cover sometimes four or five halls. It can be rather overwhelming if you don't have a plan, but I'd studied the exhibitor list and defined a few sections that I wanted to look at.

They were toys and games, jewellery, ornaments and gifts.

Over the following weeks I began ordering my stock and the smallest bedroom in the house became the storeroom. Shelves were purchased and a new business set-up was underway.

I was now making good money online and so it was time to look at other sales and distribution models to grow. So, I held a party at home just before Christmas, decking out the conservatory as my shop, and invited all my friends.

I then held an event at our daughter's nursery and had the yummy mummy brigade attend. My failure at this event was making it an 'order on the night and I'll deliver later on' model. I should have just rocked up with the stock and sold it immediately on the night. This fed into my newly emerging dislike of stockholding businesses.

My other mistake, and one that nearly landed me in a legal court case, was uploading a supplier's images to eBay. I thought as

I was selling their products it was win-win for them, so I took scans of the items from their brochure, cropped and uploaded them alongside my product listing of their items. It took an age.

A quick call a few days later from the aggrieved supplier in a firm and slightly threatening tone, the kind that makes your blood run cold, and I was taking down the images and listings with more speed than a lightning bolt on a thundery day, and I made my humble apologies. It was a harsh lesson in copyright infringement that I've never forgotten. There was no malice on my part in the slightest. It was pure naivety and what I thought was initiative. I thought there was no harm in doing what I did. I quickly learnt otherwise.

Gifts 4U UK continued for about 18 months. I ended up not enjoying it – the hours were long, the physicality of wrapping, packing, posting, restocking and housing the actual stock became a chore. I could have continued scaling, employed people, rented a premises but it was obviously not what I was supposed to be doing. Plenty of people make a huge living from eBay and I take my hats off to them! Bravo!

Athena Business Services

What's in a name?

In February 2014 I needed a name for my new business. I knew my service was going to be in the form of business consultancy and bookkeeping but was stuck on the name aspect.

Back in the day, before the world wide web made its appearance, there was a business directory called *Yellow Pages*, one published each year for every region of the country. A huge great big doorstep of a book all in yellow with black font.

If you were looking for a plumber, say, you'd go to that section and scroll down the alphabetical names until you found one you liked the sound of. Suffice to say few people would get to the back end of the alphabet, either out of frustration or boredom, so it paid to have your name starting with an 'A'.

I also wanted a name that meant something to me, and through my brainstorming I started going through Greek and Roman mythology. Not sure how I ended up there, but I did.

Athena is the Greek goddess of 'courage and wisdom' and that struck an immediate chord with me, but a goddess? Me?

Definitely not! But there was something about 'courage and wisdom' that summed up my previous three years of life-roller-coaster-riding that I connected with. Athena Business Services was born!

The other trick, by naming it 'Business Services', this meant I wasn't setting up to be a one trick pony – I could offer many things to many people. However, that's where it all got a little confusing for people once I started networking with my new proposition. I was offering bookkeeping, business consultancy and franchise consultancy... all on my own!

My aim of offering as many services as possible, hoping to attract clients from all areas, actually worked against me as people didn't know what I was truly about or selling. From a networking perspective they didn't know how to refer me. A conversation one day with Cliff Kendle from King's Lynn IT cemented what I suspected. He suggested I pick one service and promote that.

Franchising is quite niche; it doesn't suit every business and it's a high-ticket entry price for consultancy, inevitably limiting the number of prospective clients. I could do the work no problem from my experience, but would there be enough clients to work with from the pool I was networking in? I decided to go with the easier recurring revenue win of the bookkeeping service.

The business people I was networking with were more suited to that offering and I had a better chance of getting a client base up and running in line with my financial requirements. AKA, 'Get as much money coming through the door now', instead of a long pipeline of enquiries taking time to work through to sale if I'd chosen franchising.

Also, by going to work with a client at the bookkeeping level meant I had direct access to the figures of their business and could use that to leverage my consultancy skills by suggesting ways of increasing profits.

Having aligned with the Xero software as my bookkeeping tool I started promoting that too by offering discounts on the subscriptions if clients came under my practice management. The beauty of the software being cloud based was that the client and I could, along with their accountant, all have access any time we wanted. The numbers and reporting would be visible once the bookkeeping had been brought up to date.

Growing

Slowly but surely the clients started coming on board and I was off on my new business adventure. Working from home alone, as many people do to begin with, I was filing and posting receipts in the afternoon and evenings once I'd been networking and collected my daughter from school. The money started to come in and I was ok. I knew I would be all along, but there was an inevitable period of fear and uncertainty I can clearly remember.

By early 2015, almost a year in, I was beginning to become snowed under with the workload. It was time to find my first team member. I needed someone with bookkeeping experience, but I would teach them the rest: how the clients worked, as they all had their own quirks, how Xero performed, and my systems too.

Building the Athena team

After enduring a couple of not very good interview candidates, I found Martine Halls, who joined me in March 2015. We worked together until we both went our separate ways in 2022 when I relocated to Lincolnshire. It was a brilliant working relationship and Martine was a complete star! She was always reliable, hardworking, quick to process, accurate, and supportive to me. Everything I needed, she provided.

Around 2017 the client base was still growing, and I was doing more and more with my biggest client. I needed more help.

So then Karen Hurn joined the team, coinciding with deciding to rent an office in King's Lynn in the historic quarter, which is beautiful; the buildings have such wonderful character. Karen understood me and Athena immediately and it was a true alignment in timing and mutual needs.

Taking on the office was an increased expense yes, but once I started promoting the fact we had premises, I noticed a shift change in people's minds that I was actually running a viable and credible business. Funny how perceptions affect people's buying habits. I must be doing ok, I guess they thought, and I was.

Sarah Warden, who I'd met at networking, became a good friend and I outsourced her payroll services to our clients. We were now a solid team of four, getting together occasionally for meals out and our favourite afternoon teas.

My mantra with the ladies was this – that because we were all mums of primary school age children and our work was carried out on the cloud, I didn't mind when the work was done, as long as it got done. This gave us all the flexibility of working around school hours or after the kids' bedtime if we chose. It's hard fitting full-time work around young children and I knew this first hand, so I wanted to build my business model to accommodate that. It worked well and we were all happy.

Crossroads

By 2019 I was bursting at the seams and had come to a crossroads regarding where I was to go next. Continue building the bookkeeping business or join my main client full-time and sell Athena? This was such a tough decision, but I had to choose one. Was I to leave my client and build my baby or help my client build his exciting business with the boundless opportunities this offered? In the end and after much heart-felt deliberation I chose the latter. More on that later!

I had founded and grown Athena over the previous five years, and I had built a team of four and serviced many clients. I was turning over 6 figures a year and earning nicely by this time, but the constant pull in different directions from clients and the team when they needed me, was exhausting. However much I built the team with people to run it or put a manager in, there was always only one of me to go round.

I had the difficult discussion with the team and gave them first refusal on purchasing Athena. They had become invested in the brand as much as me and wanted to see it continue. After thought and discussions with their other halves, they all declined but thanked me for the opportunity, which I fully respected. It was now time to approach local accountants to offer one of them a bolt-on to their business.

By doing this I was able to sell Athena Business Services in September 2019. I then signed a full-time employment contract with my client, who was now my boss. Martine came with me and we continued sharing the same office at the business premises that we'd been working in for a while. She also kept a few of the Athena clients and serviced them herself which was good to know and continuity for my clients, staying with a familiar face.

I remember being emotional on sale day at leaving the business I had created but at the same time I knew it was the right moment to move on to bigger things. Instead of servicing multiple clients on a daily basis it was back into full-time employment to concentrate on building one business globally with one business owner and boss! I was ready!

Before consigning Athena to history, here is Karen, sharing her story of working with me and Team Athena.

Karen's story

"Nikki and I attended the same accounting course at the local college way back in the mid-90s. Our paths never crossed again until 2017 when I heard on the grapevine that she was looking for bookkeeping staff.

Without hesitation I sent over my CV and we arranged to meet. A two-hour chat later and as the saying goes… the rest *is Athena history!*

I had decided to call time on my previous role after 13 years with a local family business, but I knew the next stage had to be something unique and special, and that is exactly what I found at Athena.

I fully believed in Nikki and everything she wanted to achieve with the business – the Athena vibes and ethos were contagious. It became a labour of love for me and never felt like work, as I loved everything we did so much. The buzz I got from securing a new client was fantastic.

Nikki gave me responsibility and autonomy very early on which boosted my confidence, and my self-belief soared through the roof realising my own potential was unlimited.

Working with Nikki was empowering in a way I had not previously experienced. I learnt to take a very different approach to situations and people which I still use now in everyday life and for that I am truly grateful!

Thank you, Nikki, for believing in me and the very memorable Athena years which continually influence who I am today."

My Daughter's Story

Hannah is the apple of my eye. She is the spitting image of her dad and has my character. A natural salesperson, with the gift of the gab inherited from her father and my dad, I watch in fascination about where life and career will take her.

She has already visited a vast amount of the globe and travel is her passion.

Our mother/daughter bond is a strong one. We could at one stage read each other's minds and know what the other was going to say next, which is kinda scary now and I hope she's grown out of that little skill!

I still feel guilt at the amount of time I left her as a baby and child, choosing to work, because that's how I'm built. I think though mum-guilt (and dad-guilt for that matter) start the minute you conceive and never ends. It's just residing the whole time and no matter what you do or how hard you try to be a good parent it still speaks to you from the inner workings of your mind.

I hope I have made up for the time I spent away by treating her to fabulous holidays and trips. We did the *Sound of Music* tour in Salzburg, spent my 40th birthday together in Lake Garda and for her 20th birthday we went to Menorca with our two closest friends. One day on that trip we ventured off to the main town of Mahon and the rain started. I trotted off to find some pacamacs for us all and chose the brightest yellow ones I could find, knowing it would make everyone laugh. Newly robed in our bright plastic outfits we went off shopping. Totally unaware of what we looked like Hannah turned round to find us all and burst out in hysterics. Dotted around the ground floor of this clothes shop we looked like we'd stepped straight out of a *Minions* movie. The photos she took of that day still crack us up instantly.

For her 21st, again with our best gal-pals, we travelled to Nice in the South of France. The girls did a perfume making course, we dined in Monaco and walked the promenade in Cannes. It's those memories we have to cherish from our trips and adventures, quality over quantity, that I adore. Without working we couldn't have done all those things together. I rest easy on my decisions now as a mum.

Here Hannah shares her story about growing up in a business family...

"Growing up within a family who are career driven and passionate about what they do has meant that ultimately, I want that for myself.

My parents, aunty and grandparents have all owned their own businesses at one point since I was little, and so I have been surrounded by individuals who have had an idea and developed it into something to be proud of. I could see from early on that my granddad inspired my mum and many others, especially through his work ethic, sales technique and drive.

When my granddad was ill and becoming confused, he woke up one morning, put on his shoes and said he was off to work. He had been retired 6 years. In that moment, I understood the level to which your business can and should be your passion. To not want to retire, and if and when you do, to almost miss the thrill of it all. I can imagine my mum doing the same; the woman who never stops and who I completely admire for doing so.

My mum is someone who gravitates towards creative spaces. For her, it's looking for the next opportunity, and not stopping once you've hit your first goal. It's about understanding that challenges are an opportunity for growth and not failure. For my mum, there wasn't the option to quit, but I also know now, from venturing into a career myself, that she didn't want to. Already having one of the hardest jobs in my opinion, of being a single mum and running her own business, she wanted more for my future and most importantly hers.

But this came with sacrifices. From work trips abroad, to weekly networking events across the region, I would often have sleepovers at my nan's and became a regular at the after-school club. In the school holidays, when I was around 10 years old, my mum would often take me with her to networking events. I would pass the time by making loom-band bracelets, whilst she had 1:1s and presentations.

Looking back now, I understand that my mum was showing me her passion. She instilled a confidence in me from an early age and the independence to do the same as her in the future if I chose to. So, the loom-bands became a short-lived 'company', and I made about £20 in one day from selling these bracelets to business owners at a networking event, which to a 10-year-old was like winning the lottery.

Around this time, my granddad created a plant-selling company named after my cousins and me, where he would work endlessly throughout the summer. I would help by picking out plants and working out change to give to the customers. He taught me the value of working hard for what you want and that "You're never lost if you keep moving".

My dad has shown me the freedom which follows in owning a business, by being able to retire early. My auntie has taught me the art of balancing both personal and work life. My nan has taught me to stay proud of my achievements and to remove myself from a place that limits my potential. My mum has taught me that success comes from perseverance, creativity and commitment. But most importantly that you spend most of your life working, so why not have some fun with it?

So, despite being only twenty-one, I know, from the people around me, that the opportunities and challenges that come round the corner could have you on a plane in a week or hitting your first goal in a month. And that makes for a pretty cool story to tell!"

Part 3

Get Your Voice Heard

Introduction

Marketing is all about making people aware of you, your brand and your business on a continual basis.

Getting your voice heard is paramount to this process.

I've worked with people who I consider to be natural at this and maybe you could say are 'marketing geniuses'. They use a combination of charm, quick thinking and a constant banging of their drum to be heard.

In this chapter I would like to share their stories and introduce you to some of the greats I have had the pleasure to work and learn from, along with some personal stories of course.

We're Getting the Band Back Together

I eventually missed singing professionally and I'd always wanted to sing with a band. The opportunity arose one summer at a local primary school fundraiser. A band led by Lionel Merz was playing, and a friend, slightly tipsy, suggested I join them on stage. I did, completely unrehearsed! At the end of the night, Lionel asked if I wanted to join the band. "Based on that?" I laughed!

So I joined, and we became 'Noisy Neighbours'. The gigs started again, but this time, I was a single mum juggling a job that required travel to London. Mum helped with my daughter, and Dad supported me when he could. I loved it, but after 18 months, I bowed out. I simply had to realise that my carefree early 20s were long gone. I had different responsibilities now and could not possibly continue juggling so many plates.

Retirement, take two

I look back fondly on those singing days. We had some incredible nights with our loyal groupie friends and family. These days, my performances are limited to the occasional karaoke bar on holiday. But the presenting skills? I use them all the time!

No Boys Allowed!

"Today, ladies, our guest speaker is going to tell us the best colours to wear for maximum impact when selling."

Brilliant! (And by "brilliant," I mean sarcastically so.)

I was representing our conservatory cleaning company and trying my hand at networking as a way to find new customers. One of the local 'networking gurus' in town invited me to a 'Ladies Only' event. To be honest, I wasn't thrilled by the idea. The whole 'ladies-only' vibe didn't sit well with me, but I decided to bite the bullet and attend to see what all the fuss was about.

I walked into that event full of optimism, ready to connect with others and get to know my fellow attendees. But what I found didn't quite match my expectations. The first thing that hit me was the overall tone. It was flat and no one was really engaging. Instead, it was more about which colours were "most impactful" when selling, and what style of shoes made you look the most professional. The presenter even managed to offend one of the ladies by telling her she didn't really suit the yellow blouse she was wearing. I mean, what?

As the event went on, I couldn't shake the feeling that the entire premise of a women-only business space was limiting. I believe that real, lasting connections happen when we get out of our comfort zones. Networking shouldn't be about surrounding ourselves exclusively with people who share the same gender or experiences.

For me, the most powerful connections and learning moments come from engaging with a diverse group of individuals, regardless of gender. There's power in mixing with people who have different perspectives, experiences and insights. Limiting the space to women-only doesn't encourage that kind of diversity.

I don't particularly want to be in a room where the focus is on me being a woman in business, because I've never thought of myself that way. I want to be in a room where my expertise, ideas and capabilities speak for themselves. I have never felt held back by my gender. I work on my actions speaking louder than my words or my X and Y chromosomes.

Absolutely there is a time for girls-only events but for me that's on a weekend with my friends, out socialising, having a few drinks and giggles and sharing stories about him indoors. For business… it's a "No" from me I'm afraid!

The truth is, business networking is about building relationships based on shared interests, challenges and goals, not on gender. Whether you're a man or a woman, if you're serious about growing your business, you'll want to connect with people who have something valuable to offer.

So, next time someone invites me to a women-only event, I'm going to politely decline. Not because I don't support women, quite the opposite. It's because I don't feel the need to alienate half the population from my networking activities and I certainly don't want to be 'man-bashing' while I'm doing it, which in my experience is what happens more often than not. I find that very disrespectful and unprofessional.

I champion both men and women and want to work and connect with both. Networking should be about building strong, authentic relationships, and those relationships aren't defined by gender.

4Networking & Brad Burton

It was while attending a 4Networking event in Chelmsford, Essex, supporting one of the Cloud Bookkeeping franchisees, that I first met Brad Burton, author of the Foreword to this book. He is the founder of 4Networking, and his national network helped and supported me to grow my bookkeeping business when I set it up in 2014.

Brad is a whirlwind of energy, a marketing genius, and you definitely know when he's in the room because you can feel it. He and his networking events were like a breath of fresh air. The buzz in the room was electric and I loved 4N (as everyone calls it) from that moment on. Whatever they were all on at 8am in the morning I wanted some of it!

Brad is now on a journey of rebuilding himself after a long legal battle with an online stalker. He and I reconnected in early 2025 and I could see immediately that he had been through a shedload of trauma. He's now re-emerging as a stronger businessperson and the motivational leader we all know him to be. His has been a powerful story of determination and resilience that will propel him into new possibilities. It's so tragic that he had to experience the negatives in order to be where he is now, but I firmly believe in everything being for a reason, you just can't see it all at the time.

I needed to network

Back to February 2014, when I had set up my business on a gloomy winter's day, and looking at my shiny new website and fancy business cards, I could see I was missing a key ingredient. I had no clients and only two months' worth of money in the bank. I knew I had to get out networking and as soon as possible. So, I set about researching what was available in my area.

Not a lot, as it happens. What to do?

I'd found the network I wanted to be a part of in 4N but when I clicked on their online map there was a huge gap over the East of England. I recall the nearest group with regular meetings to me was St Neots (90 minutes away) so I duly booked in. There was also a networking meeting in Ely, which was around 40 minutes away, under a different network, BNI, but I was desperate to get going at this point so just booked into whatever I could find.

I straightaway worked out that BNI was not for me. I tried it and didn't like the structure, which I found too formal. This is an important point – if you're going to be successful in your networking you need to find a style of networking group and its people that you 'fit'.

I sent an email to 4N head office, asking whether there were plans for new groups in my area. I was quickly contacted by one of the directors, Stefan Thomas, who said he was going to put me in touch with my closest Regional Leader. He told me there had been meetings in my area but the majority of the groups running them had closed. That didn't put me off, as I was now determined to start a new 4Networking group in my area and get some meetings going. And, with this, get some money coming in.

Launching meeting #1 in King's Lynn

After I met with 4N Regional Leader Michelle Turner-Davidson in Cambridge the following week, we set about planning my first networking group launch, which was to be in my hometown of King's Lynn. I had to source the venue, and after a couple of attempts found one with a great location and free parking, just off the A47, perfectly positioned for 'Passporting' to later on. One of the things I loved about 4Networking was the way it was structured. You didn't join a single local group; you joined the whole national network, giving you the freedom to attend meetings as a 'Passport' member (each group ran them fortnightly) at any group. I got on the phone to invite all the new people I had met at my initial networking meetings to date. I managed to get a mention in the local newspaper and was contacted by Simon Hunt off the back of it, an accountant who is still a good friend to this day.

Michelle had booked Brad to come along to do the '4Sight' so the pressure was on to get as many people as possible in the room. At every 4N meeting there is a '4Sight slot', a 20-minute presentation on a business topic, which should be "an insight not a sales pitch". I think from memory we had just over 25 attend, which was a great start, and after the meeting, (after everyone had received a good 'Bradding' pep talk) we were off and away! It felt fantastic. The next meeting was in two weeks' time, but there was loads of work to do off the back of that two-hour first meeting.

Launching meeting #2 in Ely

After the success of King's Lynn, we decided to launch another 4N group, close by, in Ely. A beautiful and historic town just north of Cambridge with a stunning cathedral you can see from miles around across the Fens. Forty minutes drive from King's Lynn, it was the perfect partner meeting for King's Lynn and the two groups had a meeting on alternate weeks between the two locations.

The Ely launch was set for the beginning of April, and it was a biggie. I put 'Steve The Barman', one of my new friends and members, in as the host and Group Leader, as he already knew loads of business people in the area and had a big personality. His business was cocktails under the name of 'Thirst First' and on my first glance at his website and branding I thought it was brilliant. I thought straightaway he could be the Jamie Oliver of the cocktail world. In addition to his business, he was able to command a room and keep everyone in check.

The summer breakfast events at this venue, out on the terrace, in direct view of the cathedral, were stunning, and it became one of the best performing meetings across the country – a well-earned 'Flagship Group'. It was a 4N goldmine for membership and interaction.

Accelerated exposure

The other major benefit to running the meetings, building teams and hosting was that my profile was getting additional exposure. Not only was I Nikki Butlin of Athena Business Services, I was

Nikki Butlin, 4N Group Leader, then Area Leader looking after 8 meetings and then eventually Regional Leader looking after the three counties of Norfolk, Suffolk and Cambridgeshire, with 10–12 meetings across the whole of East Anglia.

Where there had been no 4N meetings for a significant amount of time, we built a thriving region which was topping the national leader board. And we were having a lot of fun. Evening socials with my new friends became a regular occurrence and it was great to have other people in the same boat to talk to. Running your own business can be very lonely at times and not everyone understands the pitfalls and stresses you go through each day.

There were often long days with 5am alarms (which is the middle of the night as far as I'm concerned) followed by arranging to meet with new connections and then, the most important thing, actually getting the client work that was coming in completed on my own and getting paid.

Going national

Not only did 4N run this national network of breakfast, lunch and evening meetings; they would also host national events, which my teams and I signed up for straightaway. Any chance to meet more people from our 'tribe', as Ely member and business coach Jill McCulloch once referred to 4N as, the better. Bigger stages, high profile speakers, exhibition stands for us to sell from, and an evening dinner, all further strengthened everyone's relationships. It was such a brilliant time.

A Xero fluke

At one of these national events, Gary Turner, UK Managing Director of the accounting software Xero, was speaking. Gary had been in software his whole career and had been tasked with launching Xero to the UK by its founders in New Zealand. I had first been introduced to Xero when working for Cloud Bookkeeping. For some reason, I had dismissed it to begin with but when I set up Athena and the Sage software subscriptions became too expensive and restrictive, being PC-based instead of cloud-based, I got myself trained up on Xero and then had the perfect online tool to grow with my clients.

Brad and Gary were mates, having forged a strong relationship through their businesses, and it turned out to be another great coup when I attended one of Brad's 'Be a Better Speaker' courses, as Gary had also signed up. There was a room of about 20 of us and Brad asked us all to stand at the front of the room and introduce ourselves.

I remember saying something along the lines of, "Hi, I'm Nikki and I run Athena Business Services. I can't be a natural blonde because I chose 4N for my marketing and Xero for my accounts software", pointing to Brad and Gary in turn. Everyone laughed. It was like a true alignment of people that I had magnetised to me to help me run my new venture. You can't make this stuff up! That speaking course was fantastic, and my presenting skills improved massively, learning how to tell my story in the most effective way. If you present in public in any way, a speaking course is highly recommended.

Speaking gigs

I had presented numerous 4Sights at 4N meetings by this stage and so was used to speaking in public. Plus, my background in professional singing came in handy too. So, a few months later I took the bold step and asked Brad if I could present at his upcoming 4N national leadership meeting, which he immediately agreed to. To a room of about 100 people, I told my story about starting with a sparse networking region of just two meetings within an hour of my home, to a region full of meetings, teams and opportunities. Another tick in the box of achievements and a tick in the box for exposure.

4NTV

Brad wasn't finished yet with his marketing prowess. He then launched '4NTV', a YouTube channel for 4N members, alongside Steve Hyland, who ran Business Connections Live. Again, I stepped out of my comfort zone and asked to appear, which again Brad kindly agreed to. You can still see my episode on YouTube as, with everything you do online, it lasts forever. I'm not sure I'll be watching again in a hurry as it's not the most enjoyable task watching myself on the telly box but I'm proud I did it and it increased my exposure further.

Networking post-Covid

I stepped away from my 4N roles after a couple of years, to focus on my business. On 20th March 2020 Brad's 4Networking was, as he will tell you, "wiped out overnight" due to Covid-19. The health policy to 'stay at home' was as far removed from face-to face networking as you can get. Always the quick thinker, Brad immediately took the meetings online. He has since gone on to sell the 4Networking business and now concentrates on his motivational speaking and Team Maker sessions.

As I write in 2025, the networking landscape in the UK has changed significantly post pandemic, and I still see people wary, or dare I say lazy even, to venture out and meet in person. It's a huge shame because there is no substitute for personal contact. You don't really get to know a person online. As much as the world is changing over to digital platforms, I strongly believe we should remember our roots and that people *need* social contact – it's who we are.

Captain Fawcett

I worked with Richard Finney MBE for a total of eight years. His company, Captain Fawcett, is a purveyor of the finest gentleman's grooming products, covering the globe. In its fourth year when I was first introduced to him back in 2014, side by side Richie and I combined our creative and logical skills to grow the business and the team. It was a hell of an adventure. Now we're collaborating again to share in this chapter of the book, when our lives crossed paths and were never quite the same again.

Richie has always been fabulous with words, so if you would be kind enough to indulge us, we're going to tell our story together, starting in Richie's inimitable style:

"King's Lynn, Norfolk & good

King's Lynn was once England's foremost medieval port, where merchants bartered wares under the auspices of the Hanseatic League; it is here, overlooking the River Ouse, that Captain Fawcett's first HQ was established. Outside, salty air from the Wash mingled with the occasional whiff of fish from little boats which still put out to sea each day, as they had for hundreds, if not thousands of years. Inside, the delectable scent of fresh handmade Moustache Wax mingled with strong tea, drunk in bucket loads by Yours Truly, a man seemingly forever on the brink of his next breakthrough, or, perchance, breakdown.

Indeed, I'd wager most great enterprises teeter on the edge of unbridled success and total mayhem. As such, back in June 2014 business was booming for Captain Fawcett, but, as company founder and the Captain's 'Right Hand Man', my to-do list was going completely bananas. I have a very clear idea of how things should look and sound, however, I struggle with numbers and practicality, so, having seen how companies with huge potential can implode without a firm grip on the finances, I knew it was high time Captain Fawcett engaged the services of an expert bookkeeper. Enter Nikki.

When Nikki walked into Captain Fawcett's rather delirious HQ, it was immediately clear that she wasn't just a whizz with spreadsheets. She understood, as one might say, the art of the deal. Meticulous, insightful, and unflappable, I had a notion Nikki may well be exactly the right co-pilot for Captain Fawcett's somewhat deranged ship."

Bookkeeping for the Captain

I remember clearly the first time I met Richie Finney. I was utterly taken aback by the office and the brand. I loved it from that very moment! The old-world feel of the website and the story of 'Captain Fawcett' himself "attempting to navigate to the source of the Ubangi, a major tributary to the Congo River", whereupon years later his trunk was found containing wonderful recipes for gentleman's grooming requisites. It was amazing!

So much thought and detail had already gone in, and it was like stepping back in time... I was hooked from the get-go.

After the initial tour, Richie said he needed a bookkeeper. The classic entrepreneurial journey from startup to initial stages of growth, when you simply cannot do everything yourself anymore.

I knew, with multi-currency activity and an online shop as well as commercial sales, it was not going to be a small amount of work each month. I went back to see Richie the following week and put my proposal forward.

To say he almost fell off his chair in reaction to my detailed cost proposal is an understatement (Oh no I thought!). I was early on in my client acquisition process, or in layperson terms, I was desperate for some income! However, I knew the level of work involved and the value of my services, so I stuck to my guns. It would have been extremely easy to have been so enamoured with the business model, brand, and my own personal circumstances, to have undersold my service.

So, I told him politely that he had my contact details should he change his mind, and I got up to leave. He came out with me to the car park; we chatted some more and shook hands on the deal I had proposed.

"Monaco or Bust

In January 2016, Captain Fawcett was sponsoring a dear friend at the legendary Monte Carlo Rally – Per Simble, my brother in the wind, now gone to ride the endless road. This was a high-

stakes, high-octane event... big opportunities, big decisions, big price tags. And here it became apparent Nikki was so much more than Captain Fawcett's 'Bean Counter'.

Stepping out, dressed to the nines at a black-tie dinner, she was both a superbly glamorous ambassador for the Captain Fawcett brand and, with a weather eye on the purse strings, always making sure every penny was spent wisely. Well, except for the ice creams. Some expenses are quite simply non-negotiable."

Yes Richie, I remember it well, the trip of a lifetime and we dared to call it 'work'!

It was during the end of the 5-day race whilst getting ready for that sumptuous black-tie dinner, when it suddenly hit me.

The date.

It was 3rd February.

Exactly two years to the day since I had started Athena Business Services. I kid you not. You could not have made it up!

Two years since I had sat at home, with no clients, just a laptop, an idea, and two months' worth of savings in the bank, wondering if I would even make it.

And now?

Now, I was in Monaco, getting ready to dine in Monte Carlo. Working on a project I never could have foreseen. Surrounded by incredible people who had become wonderful friends.

It was one of those rare moments when life forces you to pause and acknowledge how far you have come.

I stood there for a second, just letting it sink in. Two years.

It's funny, isn't it?

You take a leap. You say yes to the right opportunities. You push through the doubts. And suddenly, you find yourself miles away from where you started, sometimes quite literally.

Berlin Wall

Captain Fawcett conducted a huge amount of business overseas, its largest market being Europe. Often, we would be on back-to-back video calls throughout the day, talking to distributors, and Richie would travel extensively without hesitation wherever he was needed.

On this particular occasion I was invited to accompany him to Berlin, Germany for an in-person meeting that required my skills.

"By June 2017, Nikki had fully evolved from financial wizard to co-strategist. She wasn't simply balancing the books. Calm, measured, and always at least three steps ahead, she understood the direction Captain Fawcett needed to go, helping to pull my occasionally wild and woolly thinking into actionable shape, always exercising the rare ability to see problems looming large, and head 'em off at the pass."

I recall this meeting not being the easiest of conversations, but Richie was great at always adding in some 'fun and adventure time' to all his trips. This one was no exception. Once business matters had concluded we were in a taxi heading straight to the Berlin Wall. I love history and Richie is so passionate about all things historical.

And the winner is…

When you're a small company and want to have a big voice, you need to use all the resources available to create the noise. This is what Richie is so great at. So, we would often enter awards. There is a huge amount of work involved in the application process – facts, figures, testimonials and such like. We would spend hours ensuring our entry was the best it could be, then keep our fingers crossed…

"In January 2019, I was delighted to share a tremendous moment. Captain Fawcett won the King's Lynn Mayor's Small Business Award, a galvanising acknowledgment of our growing success. Nikki's parents and daughter were present at a fantastic gala dinner, so amid huge applause as Captain Fawcett's win was announced, I was determined to acknowledge her key role in what had become a truly extraordinary team. Naturally, I called Nikki up on stage to take a bow, proud to stand alongside a magnificent colleague and tireless cheerleader for all we'd achieved thus far…"

India

During 2019 I accompanied Richie on a business trip to Mumbai in India. With some assistance from the Department for International Trade we signed up for a cosmetics exhibition in the city and flew out for a week.

It was a fabulous trip and working in a different country was a revelation. We had participated in many exhibitions in the UK, where you would usually arrive the day before opening, the stands ready to be set up.

India did things slightly differently, as we quickly realised. We arrived the day before with the boxes of goods that had been couriered out in advance, to find the exhibition halls still requiring carpets, some painting and cleaning. It was a mess!

Never ones to be deterred, we did as much as we could in 30+ degree heat, as the air conditioning had not yet been turned on, and then had to wait. There was little else we could do.

The following morning, we arrived with about two hours to go until opening, to the smell of fresh paint and freshly laid carpets. There was dust everywhere and we still had to set the products out. Richie grabbed some guy and would not let him go until he had given him his hoover, it was hilarious. I managed to find a woman with a duster and some polish. We pulled out the stops as we always did and opened on time. Hoorah!

"The Trouble with Tuk-tuks

Have you ever taken a tuk-tuk ride through Mumbai traffic? Imagine strapping yourself to a rocket-powered shopping cart driven by a cove who clearly does not believe in the laws of physics or mortality, as he guns the tiny engine into a high-speed demolition derby choreographed by a lunatic god. Gadzooks! Would I even have survived without Nikki's steadying presence?! Suffice to say, she is a trooper, who has a just brilliant way of adapting to different environments and cultures. Her calm ability to reveal order in chaos helped build the sustainable foundations of Captain Fawcett's ambitious global growth."

Fawcett on brand

Richie eats, sleeps and breathes Captain Fawcett, still to this day. When others around him are retiring he is still the first one in the building and often the last one to leave. He works every day and is as sharp as a tack. A wordsmith and creative, his energy would put the youngest and fittest person to shame.

While out in public he will always be seen in his trademark brown coat, in his persona of the 'Captain's Right-Hand Man'. He would always say, "The Captain is a refined Edwardian Gentleman and I'm a tubby biker, no one would believe I was him", to which we would all chuckle.

I often thought he was not doing himself any favours by putting himself front and centre of his brand the whole time, but I realise now, he is the Key Person of Influence for his company. He is the voice and relatable character at the front, one of the leaders in his industry and disrupting it along the way as every entrepreneur should do. I worried that he was doing too much, that other people should take on some of the responsibilities, but he was insistent, and you cannot bend that force of resilience when it's so strong.

"In the Limelight

Nikki was never just behind the scenes. From the off, she was a true Captain Fawcett Ambassador Extraordinaire. By Jove, this woman can talk shop with anyone! And she does it with effortless charm, a cracking sense of humour and simply impeccable sense of style! She always rocked up at events with a perfect retro twist, 1940s' waves and all.

September 2019 marked a milestone, a turning point for Captain Fawcett and also for me personally. Nikki stepped on board full-time and that's when I knew we could take things further and faster. In truth, it was a huge relief. Captain Fawcett had outgrown part-time solutions, and, as such I hugely valued the assurance of Nikki's confident hand on the wheel.

Planes, Trains, Automobiles... and Whatever Gets You There Alive

There were a multitude of magnificent moments in Monaco, Mumbai and Mallorca; private jets, mad dashes for trains, the occasional helicopter ride, a rather swanky yacht... and, somewhere in the middle of it all, an immense amount of stupendously hard work, with trade shows in Harrogate, the NEC, Olympia and more. It was all part of the veritable whirlwind that defines working with Captain Fawcett.

Throughout everything, Nikki remained a stalwart logistical mastermind. By keeping the finances on track, she allowed the brilliant marketing team, and of course Yours Truly, to forge ahead with creative, imaginative, and on occasion unhinged, fervour. Nikki made sure we got where we needed to be in one piece, and that it all made financial sense to boot!"

Brexit, Covid, and running out of steam

By the end of 2021, after dealing with Brexit and latterly Covid, where Richie had been really poorly, I was exhausted and burnt out. I felt I had done as much as I could for his company to take it forward, and I needed a new challenge. In addition to this, my new partner lived in Lincolnshire, and I was spending more and more time up there. Everything was coming to a head.

It was time for me to move on and find someone new to help. To bring my skills to a new table and add value with the experience I had clocked up. I knew Richie would benefit from a fresh pair of eyes and some renewed energy to drive him to the next level.

"The Hardest Goodbye

March 2022, Nikki decided it was time for her to move on. A bittersweet moment, to say the very least. On one hand, I was immensely proud of her for taking the next step. On the other, I had to face the somewhat alarming reality of keeping Captain Fawcett on an even keel without her. But Nikki, quite simply, is a real pro. Before heading off, she made sure she left the business in pristine order. Thanks to everything she'd put in place, Captain Fawcett's story could carry on without her, albeit with the necessity of 'Keeping A Stiff Upper Lip Regardless'.

Nikki, I am eternally grateful. For your support, your wisdom, your friendship, and, of course, for making sure Captain Fawcett was never completely bankrupted by extravagant ordering of impromptu ice creams. Things simply would not be the same without you.

Together, we grew Captain Fawcett from a promising venture into something bigger, wilder, and way more exciting than either of us could ever have predicted. It was an utterly mad, exhilarating ride, part business, part adventure, all completely unbelievable!

All in all, Nikki was a most highly esteemed colleague, and she will always remain a very dear chum. She played her part, then spread her wings, cut loose, and away she flew.

Huzzah!"

Richard Finney MBE

We both cried a lot of tears on my final day, and I'm so pleased we are still in contact to this day.

In the 2025 New Year's Honours, Richie was awarded an MBE for Services to Trade and Charity; I was so thrilled for him! What an achievement and so well deserved.

I am truly grateful that I met this man, and the adventures we had together. It was incredibly tough on occasions but we both came out the other side in one piece with skills and stories to share. Most importantly, we made some fabulous memories of our time working together.

I raise a glass to you Dear Chum!

Part 4

Team Is Everything

Introduction

I've done both, working alone and working in a team. And without question, I much prefer the latter.

When you work alone, the weight of every decision, every challenge, and every opportunity, falls solely on your shoulders. It can be isolating, overwhelming, and sometimes even paralysing. There's no one to bounce ideas off, no fresh perspectives, and no support when things get tough. You're the only motivator, problem solver, strategist and executor. It's exhausting.

But when you have a team, everything changes.

A strong team is more than just a group of people working

towards a common goal; it's a powerhouse of collaboration, innovation and resilience. The ability to share ideas, problem-solve collectively and support one another, is priceless. It's the difference between struggling in silence and thriving through shared knowledge and effort.

Think about it. Some of the most successful businesses in the world didn't rise to the top because of one person alone. They got there because of a team, people who believed in the mission, challenged each other to grow, and combined their strengths to achieve something bigger than themselves.

Business is full of highs and lows. A team provides a safety net, a group of people who can lift you up when things get tough and celebrate your wins with you. There's a level of accountability and encouragement that just doesn't exist when you're working solo.

Two (or more) heads are always better than one. Having people around you to offer fresh perspectives, challenge your thinking, and provide solutions you might not have considered, can be the game-changer your business needs.

When you work alone, there's only so much you can do in a day. With a team, tasks get done faster, ideas turn into action quicker, and progress happens at a much faster pace. Time is one of the most valuable assets in business, so why not maximise it with a strong team?

Joining ASC Metals

At the end of 2021 I needed a change.

Exhaustion, frustration, and the acknowledgement that I had done as much as I could for Captain Fawcett. It was time for someone else to bring in fresh eyes, fresh energy, and take it to the next level. My time there was coming to an end.

Manifesting change

I set about looking for a new position and true to form I wrote down what I wanted from my next dream role. It's funny, because when I moved house in 2022, I found the piece of paper detailing my wishes. Almost every single one of them was fulfilled by ASC Metals in Lincoln where I now hold the role of Finance Director.

I knew I wanted to join a bigger company than I'd worked with before. What's the point of moving if you don't step outside your comfort zone and push to grow your skills and knowledge further?

I knew that although I didn't have a formal accountancy qualification, I had enough experience of running finance departments in SMEs and working alongside the company accountant to do the role justice. That's the kind of confidence you get when you've been doing something for a long time. An awareness of your own strengths and weaknesses and where you can add value.

I also had a plethora of skills in my toolkit. Not only was I experienced in finance, I had done sales, marketing, HR, operations and logistics. What I lacked in formal training I more than made up for in multiple skills.

A recruitment consultant contacted me about one job that I took an interest in. It wasn't exactly right but I thought I had nothing to lose by applying and subsequently going for an interview, which post-Covid took place online. I knew ultimately the company wasn't the right fit and I'm a firm believer in everything being for a reason when they politely declined my application.

Confidence in my convictions

Then I came across the advert for Finance Director ASC Metals Lincoln. I read the role description and the requirements, and I knew I could do everything needed. So, I applied, and I followed up my CV submission with a covering letter to the recruiter Paul Burchett, who was the current FD and retiring from the role.

A few anxious days went by and then Paul responded, asking for a telephone chat. We had a really good conversation and I told him I could do everything required except for the formal accountancy part. He responded that it didn't matter, as they had an external accountant who took care of the formal parts. Something told me this was going to be 'my role' and I decided

I was going to do everything I could to secure it.

So, I patiently waited again while Paul relayed the candidates to the Managing Director Richard Hoole. I was invited to meet with Paul and Richard at a country hotel in between our locations one evening the following week. Both men were really friendly, and I felt we all got along well. I asked plenty of questions, as is my curious nature, and I answered each of theirs with confidence and honesty. All was going well so far.

When I was invited to visit the premises and meet with Richard on his own, he showed me around the warehouse. Well, it was like stepping back into my parents' double-glazing factory. The smells, the machinery noises, the racks as high as the buildings, stacked with products, it immediately felt like home. Richard and I got along well too. This was going to be very important, as I was potentially coming in as his Finance Director, sitting right next to him on the board, helping to run the company. We had to get on. Any initial personality clashes or bad vibes would stop the process in its tracks, for me too you understand. I could not have joined a company where I didn't like the person I was to work with the closest.

It transpired that I was down to the final two, so I assured Richard that I was very interested in the position but that he had to follow his instincts. He remarked that it was going to be a difficult decision. The other candidate had the accountancy qualification, but I had more commercial experience and acumen. Tough choice.

Luckily, he got it right and chose me!!

Stepping up

I started my ASC Metals adventure on 14th March 2022. One of the things I really admired and respected from the outset was the length of service many of the team had clocked up. A business that had been founded by Richard's father Tony and had been operating for almost 40 years, some of the team had been there for 30 years, it was astounding. There aren't many places you come across like that these days. I knew they must be doing something right.

My primary role was looking after the money, and I firstly needed to learn the company's financial operations from Paul who was retiring in two months' time. Eek! The pressure was on, and I had to get it right. ASC was turning over in excess of £13m at that time and little old me was now going to be in charge of looking after the pennies. It was a huge responsibility but one that I was ready for.

Luckily, the systems were already strong and accounts practices are pretty similar in most organisations, but every business has its quirks, it's those things you have to learn. I could see pretty quickly the areas where I could add value with my reporting skills and love of spreadsheets.

Julie, who had been with the company for over 20 years, was the accounts assistant and to be honest she did most of the day-to-day processing. So, there was little in the way of those tasks for me to pick up on, which was great. Julie was hilarious, had a quick wit and was great on the telephone with the customers. She left me able to concentrate on the bigger picture and help Richard grow the business further.

Getting to know you

Once I'd nailed the finances, my next priority was getting to know the team. I'd been handed the HR baton too on arrival, which was fine as I'd done it before, so I wanted to meet with everyone individually and see what they were all about. People are always such an important factor in any business and with the track history and length of service I was keen to find out what the secret was.

I quickly discovered many differing personalities, as you would expect with a team of 35. Some were quiet, some were bold, some were new, some were established and heading into retirement phase. If you can learn about a person, their background, home life, their motivations and what makes them tick you can help them develop and grow massively in a team, in the business they work in and potentially in life too. That was my mission.

I discovered some tensions in a few places, some frustrations in others, but on the whole everyone liked and respected Richard and were pro the company and its future. Richard's father Tony had passed away the summer before I joined so I never got the chance to meet him. From my understanding he was working right up until he could physically no longer attend the office, was hands on and knew everything that was going on. A true entrepreneur of my dad's generation who worked hard, reaped the rewards but never took his foot off the gas.

Instincts flagging up red

The company had one other branch based in Leeds, that Richard had purchased a few years prior. At the end of April, he took me up to visit the team. My first impressions here were somewhat different to the Lincoln head office. There was a completely different vibe, and something was 'off' but I wasn't quite sure what. My instincts were flagging up red like no one's business.

Once back in the office and for the next month or so I began consolidating all the information I had to hand on the business. I charted the historical sales and profits against recent activity and by branch. The company had been experiencing some incredibly high trading activity off the back of Covid-19 and were doing exceptionally well. Metals are commodities and their prices fluctuate across the world due to supply and demand. The supply chains across Europe had closed due to Covid and UK companies were being forced to purchase from further afield, which resulted in a shortage here, pushing prices up.

When I broke the figures down by branch however, the Leeds area hadn't been contributing at the same level as the Lincoln branch. My immediate question was, why not? If we were selling the same stock at the same prices in the same market, we should therefore be seeing similar proportional activity surely? But no. Something just didn't feel right. Turns out my instincts were bang on.

We closed the Leeds branch in November that year. A whole summer of events to the negative, which I'm not able to share fully, cemented our decision to shut it down and find a new tenant for the lease. Despite my best efforts, from my office 60 miles away,

I couldn't break the negative culture that had existed long before my time. From Richard's perspective it was very difficult for him to see the wood for the trees when he was stood in the forest. For me, coming in from the outside with fresh eyes, it was clearer. Between us, which has always been the case since we've worked together, we discussed, deliberated and arrived at the same conclusion.

Wanting to keep the Yorkshire customer base, but without the additional overhead, we managed to keep two members of the Leeds team, who merged with the Lincoln branch, and all of a sudden after a lot of stress it felt like one company for the first time since I'd arrived. Where there had been a 'them and us', now it was just 'us'.

When life is running in parallel

2022 was one of the hardest years of my career and my life, as it happens, because our darling dad and Mum's husband of over 50 years, passed away after a short battle with cancer, while we were in the midst of the Leeds branch redundancies. I took two weeks out of the office to help my mum and sister care for him at home in his final days, as he had wanted. I would connect with Richard every day just to stay in the loop with everything. I'm so thankful he allowed me the time and space to be where I needed to be, without question or guilt.

The week after Dad's passing, my partner and I moved house. It was a hell of a first year, but again my skill set had increased and my resilience to difficulties was unwavering. My core instincts and determination had been required in full to get the job done and thankfully they didn't let me down.

When I look back, in the space of 18 months I had relocated, started a new job, moved house twice, gone through a branch closure, redundancies, and lost my father, oh and just to add fuel to the fire the symptoms of 'a woman of a certain age' were starting to kick in. I defy anyone to come out of that little lot bright and breezy!

The newly strengthened team

Once we'd finished dealing with the difficult ramifications of the branch closure we again focused on our team. Every business, no matter its size, generally operates within the same core departments: Marketing, Sales, Operations, HR, and Finance. In micro-businesses, one or two people often juggle all these roles. In most SMEs, however, these functions are handled by dedicated teams, each with their own managers and responsibilities.

Despite ASC Metals' already impressive success, one area stood out immediately where I felt there was a gap, and that was marketing. Although the company was hugely successful, there was very little activity, especially online. I thought they were missing a trick, and if we could increase the awareness even further then we would grow the sales too.

A LinkedIn page had been set up but was dormant, customer communications were infrequent, and video content was non-existent. So, I took action. I revived the LinkedIn page, refreshing the content and posting regularly. We captured video content from the warehouse and launched a YouTube channel. Then, having organised the customer database and uploaded it to

MailChimp, I sent out ASC Metals' first company newsletter. For the first couple of months, I managed these new channels myself, getting a feel for what worked and how our audience responded. But as the workload grew, I quickly realised I couldn't, and shouldn't, do it alone.

The power of teamwork

Instead of hiring externally, I looked within the business. Who better to contribute than the team members who already knew the company, the customers and the industry inside out? I formed a Marketing Team, bringing together members from different departments, and we started meeting every 6–8 weeks to make plans, brainstorm ideas, and more importantly, delegate tasks so that no single person was overloaded.

With the right training and a clear plan, everyone got involved. Some took charge of LinkedIn, others helped with email campaigns, and we all contributed to video content. It wasn't about adding extra work to their plates – it was about giving them ownership and empowering them to shape the company's online presence.

By the end of the year, the impact was undeniable. Our LinkedIn followers grew organically from 250 to 950, YouTube views hit 500-plus on some videos, our email database expanded, and engagement rates improved significantly.

That's teamwork in action and for any business, big or small, it's the key to sustainable growth.

Richard's Story

Richard and I have worked together for over three years now at ASC Metals, as Managing Director and Finance Director respectively. We have a great working relationship, which is fundamental to the running of the company.

Here Richard shares his story…

"For years, running a business like ASC Metals meant I was used to wearing many hats. Like many business owners, I was involved in everything. It wasn't that I didn't have a great team; I did. But at that higher level, there were gaps that meant every problem and challenge ultimately landed on my desk.

My father and I had a close working relationship but, as with any family run business, there were often differences of opinion. He had an old-school way of doing things and I wanted to progress the company into the future. There was a distinct difference of opinion when I wanted to introduce a Finance Director to the team. My father was completely opposed to the idea but with some heated persuasion I managed to convince him it was a good idea and we recruited Paul Burchett.

With Paul's experience and expertise, the gaps in the team were *quickly fixed and it felt like a new chapter for ASC.*

At the end of 2021, when Paul told me he wanted to retire, I tasked him with finding his replacement. I needed the right person to step in and take the weight off my shoulders now that my father had passed away. Nikki joined the business in March 2022.

Initially, her role as Finance Director was of course focused on the numbers, but it quickly became clear that she could do much more. From the outset, she got stuck in, not just on the finances, but she helped me with strategy and operations and made it her priority to get to know the team.

After a couple of months, once Nikki had got a firm grip on the cash flow, and monthly management reports were giving me greater clarity and visibility on all areas of the business, she moved on to building a stronger marketing presence, ensuring we weren't just a great business but a visible one.

One of the biggest transformations Nikki brought wasn't just within the business, it was for me personally. For years, ASC Metals had been a huge responsibility, especially after losing my father. For a long while I was reluctant to take any time off at all. That changed when Nikki came in because I knew she was capable of looking after the company in my absence, alongside the existing team who are brilliant and know what they're doing.

With stronger financial systems, a clear marketing strategy, and a more structured leadership team, the business was no longer reliant on me being involved in every detail. For the first time in years, I could step away and know things would keep running smoothly. It's meant peace of mind for me and that, as any business owner will tell you, is priceless."

Work Yourself Out First

I'm happy being second-in-command and working in partnership.

It's taken me 30 years to work it out but it's where I'm most comfortable and happy. I've worked in my family firm alongside my Finance Mum and Entrepreneur Dad. I've run my own business and sold it. I've been self-employed as a one-woman band, and a Managing Director of a Limited Company employing staff. The top seat is not where I'm most at home, but I've had to do the top job to discover that.

Maybe it's because my parents had their own business from when I was 10 years old, and I felt I had something to prove. Maybe I don't like being told what to do by a boss; I definitely don't like that actually. Or something else, I don't know.

What I do know is that sitting right next to the MD, Owner or Founder, running the finances, advising and supporting on business strategy, looking after the team and anything else that is required of me in my role responsibility, is where I excel.

Having a sounding board to bounce ideas off and shared responsibility on decisions has been fantastic for my confidence and career progression.

No longer do I carry out 80-hour weeks, no longer do I work evenings, no longer do I work weekends. All this is my choice and I know others thrive on that workload, but for me I can truly say for the first time in a long time I have the perfect work/life balance.

They say it's lonely at the top and boy are they right! I've often heard team members complaining about their boss; the lack of time spent at their desk, excessive travel and the fancy car outside. This is often fuelled by bitterness and jealousy and a complete lack of understanding of the responsibilities of running a business.

When you have 15, 20, 50 or 100 people on your payroll and their salaries and mortgages in your hands that's a heavy burden to bear. Don't get me wrong, as a Director sat on a multi-million-pound company board I still feel those responsibilities, but they're shared and I don't go home at night unable to sleep because a decision I've made could jeopardise all of that. I sleep quite soundly now and enjoy my weekends, which is the right thing for me.

And the Oscar for Actress in a Supporting Role goes to... Me!

Build the Gaps Around You

The key to successful team building

As your business grows, so does the complexity of running it. And one of the most important aspects of growth is recognising the gaps that exist in your current team. You might be a great visionary or a strong leader, but that doesn't mean you're skilled in every area of your business. Identifying where those gaps are and filling them with the right people is a crucial step to taking your business to the next level. I've done this numerous times.

So, how do you go about plugging the gaps around you?

Identifying the skill gaps

The first step is figuring out where you sit in the business jigsaw puzzle. Take a step back and look at your strengths and weaknesses. What tasks do you avoid because they drain your energy or aren't within your skill set? For example, if you're great at managing operations but find chasing overdue payments or balancing the books tedious and stressful, then you may need some help with finance skills.

Similarly, if marketing feels like an endless maze and you're unsure how to position your brand or utilise social media effectively, it's time to admit that this is another area where you could use support. Understanding where you lack expertise and experience is the first step in identifying where to hire or seek help.

Attracting the right talent

Once you've recognised your gaps, the next step is finding the right people to fill them. You need to attract talent that not only possesses the skills you're missing but also aligns with your company's values and culture. This requires a clear job description that outlines the specific responsibilities, qualifications and expectations.

Look for people who bring a fresh perspective to the table but also share your commitment to the business. Whether you're hiring a finance person to chase debtors or a marketing expert to take your brand to new heights, ensure that the person you bring on board is someone you can trust to handle their area of expertise with minimal oversight.

Integrating new team members

Bringing new people into your business is more than just a simple hire; it's about integrating them into your team in a way that doesn't disrupt the culture you've worked so hard to build. A clear, supportive work environment is critical for productivity and for ensuring your employees want to stay. A new person can unsettle the crew to begin with while everyone works out the fit. The best way to assist in this transition period I find is with communication.

Talk to the existing team, explain where the new person is going to slot in. Assure them there's nothing to fear, talk about their own strengths and how they can help the process by taking the new person under their own wing too. Encouraging mentoring from senior and experienced members is a brilliant way to smooth the process.

By communicating that everyone is on the same team, the stronger they all work together and support each other will create a massively positive impact. Honestly, when you get this working well as a leader, it makes your business unstoppable.

Delegating tasks effectively

Delegating tasks to new team members might seem like a daunting process, especially if you're used to doing everything yourself. But once you've brought the right people on board, it's essential to trust them with responsibilities that align with their skill set. Start by assigning clear, manageable tasks, and provide them with the support and resources they need to succeed.

This is a biggie... Do not micro-manage! Trust any new employees to do what they're best at. Give them the freedom to solve problems and take initiative while providing regular feedback to ensure they're on track. The more you delegate, the more you free yourself to focus on higher-level planning and growth.

Assessing the effectiveness of new people

Once your new team members are in place, you'll need to assess their effectiveness regularly. Conduct periodic check-ins to evaluate progress and results. Are they meeting expectations? Are there areas for improvement?

Tracking their performance through measurable outcomes, such as customer satisfaction levels, sales, or productivity, can help you determine if they're a good fit. Continuous feedback, both positive and constructive, ensures that the team remains aligned and continues to grow as a strong unit.

Building your business is a journey, and it's crucial to surround yourself with the right people who can fill the gaps around you. Don't be afraid to admit where you need help – no one is good at everything (even me!). By recognising your strengths, identifying gaps, and hiring the right people to fill those gaps, you can take your business to new heights and create a strong, collaborative team that will drive success.

Keys to Recruiting

Recruiting isn't easy. No matter how polished a CV looks or how well an interview goes, you won't truly know how someone will perform until they're in the job. Even recruitment agencies can only make an educated guess.

Over the years, I've recruited fantastic people by following one key principle – knowing exactly what I need before starting. This means understanding not just the skills I need for that role but the character that fits the team.

I won't be giving you a step-by-step guide here, as there are professionals far better qualified to assist in that area. I merely want to share how I go about recruiting, to help you on your way.

- **Know who you want first and define your requirements:** It's easier to search when you know who you're searching for. Write down your wish list of attributes, what you do and don't want.

- **Self-advertise or use an agency:** This very much depends on the time and budget you have available. I've done both in varying different situations.

- **Interview your shortlist:** The best candidates ask thoughtful questions and show genuine interest in your company. They've done their research on you, which shows initiative and curiosity, which I like.

- **Skills, knowledge + character for the win:** If I've shortlisted someone for interview, it's because they read well on paper and have ticked most of my requirements. Now in interview, I want to see their character. Ask me questions and not just about the pay and the holiday entitlement! Show you want the role and are curious about the business you may be about to work for. Show who you are. If you have the basic foundations, you can be taught the rest, as long as you show enthusiasm and engagement.

- **Making the final decision:** Beyond skills, knowledge and character it's then down to trusting your instincts. Will this person add value beyond just ticking boxes? Recruitment isn't an exact science, but with clarity and intuition, you can build a strong team that drives your business forward.

People Issues

I firmly believe that people are a business's greatest asset, but sometimes they can also be my biggest challenge and headache. Whether you're an HR professional, business owner or manager, people issues are inevitable. Different personalities, opinions and emotions can create tension, but handling problems early is key. Here are my key tips.

Spotting and addressing issues early

- **Don't ignore tension.** Small frustrations escalate if left unchecked.

- **Get to the root cause.** What's visible isn't always the real issue.

- **Listen.** People want to feel heard, even if a solution isn't immediate.

- **Act quickly.** The longer conflict lingers, the worse it gets.

- **Find a resolution.** Fix it if you can or seek HR/legal guidance.

Dealing with difficult employees

Inevitably, sometimes certain individuals will naturally challenge the team dynamic. In these cases, I would:

- **Be direct.** Address the issue head-on and let them know the impact they are having.

- **Offer support.** Show them your findings but then give them a chance to improve.

- **Take action if necessary.** One person must not be allowed to derail your culture! This is incredibly important or else it can have damaging knock-on-effects on the rest of the team.

Most importantly, ensure you have good legal advice on hand when you need it, and don't make rash decisions that could land you in hot water further down the line. Finally, take a measured and calm approach, look at the facts and always act in good faith.

They are your team – look after them all the best way you can.

Part 5

Money! Money! Money!

Introduction

I've been working in business finance roles my whole career. It's at the heart of my skill set.

I fell into it quite by accident through working with my parents, wanting to find an area of the business where I could add value, but I've never ever wanted to be an accountant. I still don't to this day!

What I love is the business aspect that having a handle on the finances gives me. I love nothing more than getting a grip on the numbers and statistics (with my trusty spreadsheets in tow of course) and then working on the business strategy and planning.

I would love to now share my money stories with you. I hope you find some key takeaways.

Keep Your House in Order

I believe that in business, and in life for that matter, financial responsibility is essential. If we all take proper care of our own cash flow, pay our bills on time, chase outstanding payments promptly, and plan large expenditures sensibly, the whole system will run far more efficiently.

Too many businesses get caught in a cycle of poor financial management, and the ripple effect is huge.

If your customers pay you on time, you have the cash to pay your suppliers on time. That supplier, in turn, can pay their staff and invest in their business. It's a chain reaction that keeps everything moving.

When businesses delay payments, it causes unnecessary strain. Suddenly, people are having to chase debts, dip into reserves, or rely on credit just to keep things running. Worst case? You end up taking customers to court, filing CCJs, and reputations get damaged. Nobody wins in that scenario.

Then there's the stress. The late-night worry. The frustration of knowing you've done the work, delivered the goods, but now you're waiting weeks, sometimes months, to get paid. And when you're struggling to balance your own accounts, this trickles down. Staff don't get their bonuses, growth plans get put on hold, and small businesses, especially the ones living hand-to-mouth, end up failing. I find it heartbreaking!

But here's the thing – it doesn't have to be that way!

What if we all committed to managing our finances properly? If every business took responsibility for paying what they owe, when they owe it, and expected the same in return? No more firefighting. No more scrambling to cover last-minute gaps. No more businesses folding simply because they couldn't get paid on time.

Surely, if we all operated like this, financial stress in business would be dramatically reduced. Instead, we'd have stronger businesses and healthier cash flow.

Good financial management isn't just about keeping the lights on; it's about building something sustainable. And it starts with taking control of your own numbers, leading by example, and expecting others to do the same.

So, let's stop making excuses, stop normalising bad financial habits, and start running our businesses the way they should be run – responsibly, sustainably, and with respect for the people we work with.

Numbers Tell a Story

I can look at a set of accounts and, with a quick glance at the headline figures, get a pretty good idea of the financial health of that business. The numbers tell a story, one of stability, struggle, or growth.

I can instantly see the cash position, what's owed, what's outstanding, and whether the company is making a profit. All these things paint a clear picture of a company's strength, long before anyone utters a word about how well things are "going".

If numbers, spreadsheets and financial management aren't your strong suit, find someone who thrives in that space. They will be your right hand when it comes to looking after the money, ensuring everything is tracked, managed, and under control.

Understanding the basics

Even if accounts and reports make your eyes glaze over, you should still know how to read the headlines. It's easier than you think. At the very least, ask someone to walk you through what key figures mean and how to interpret them. You don't need to be an accountant, but you do need to understand your financial position.

Get an accounting system now!

If you're not already using accounting software, change that today. Xero is my go-to recommendation, but if that's not an option, at least set up a structured spreadsheet. Having an up-to-date system on a computer, not a pile of paper receipts, is non-negotiable.

Stay in control, even if you outsource

If handling money still really isn't your thing, then please, please, please take on someone who loves balancing bank accounts and ensures the bills are paid on time. Then, make sure they report to you at least once a week with:

- Your bank balance(s)
- What's owed to you
- What you owe to suppliers

This keeps you informed without being overwhelmed. You need to have a clear handle on the numbers, while letting your finance person manage the day-to-day details.

Keep an eye on your bank accounts

Even if you're not directly handling your financial accounts, always keep an eye on your bank accounts. If something looks off, ask. Never assume. The best business owners always know where they stand financially.

This is the approach I've taken in every business I've worked with, and I've loved it. At any moment, if a business owner wants to know their financial position, I can pull up my reports and provide an instant, accurate snapshot, including forecasts for the near future.

Cash Flow Mastery

I love the term cash flow!

When I'm asked to explain what it actually means, I like to keep it simple – no corporate jargon or techy nonsense (urgh!).

Imagine money flowing around us like water...

Sometimes, there's a flood of it. Other times, a drought. Sometimes, streams divert the flow away from us, and sometimes, leaks appear, draining it without us even noticing.

We all have our buckets, otherwise known as our bank accounts, that we want full to the brim with fresh, flowing water (cash). Just as humans need water to survive, businesses need cash to keep running. As they say, "Cash is King!"

Now, look around. Some people always seem to have overflowing buckets; in fact, they have multiple buckets going at once. Meanwhile, others have just one bucket with a slow trickle coming in, but the water leaks out just as fast. Then, at the end of the month... empty bucket!

So, what are the people with the full buckets doing differently?

They are controlling the flow, it's as simple as that.

Bossing your cash flow

1. **Maximise the flow in**

   You need multiple taps feeding your bucket; diverse revenue streams that bring in steady, reliable income. The more taps you have, the stronger your cash flow.

2. **Control the flow out**

   Install valves that release cash only when necessary. Delay payments strategically in line with payment terms, ensure expenses are well-timed, and keep a close eye on what's going out. The longer you hold onto your money, the better.

3. **Check for leaks**

   Small, unnoticed leaks can drain your cash over time. These could be old subscriptions you no longer use, unnecessary expenses, or inefficient processes. A few pounds here and there might not seem like much, but over a year, it adds up! Plug the leaks and keep checking for new ones.

Only when you have full control over these elements can you ensure that your buckets stay full and even overflow each month.

Forecasting – Predicting your cash flow

Think of cash flow forecasting like predicting the weather.

We have a general idea of how spring, summer, autumn and winter will behave weather-wise, just like we can estimate our income and expenses over time. The closer we get to a specific period of time, the more accurate our forecast becomes. Just like the weather. Clever hey?

Step 1: Log what you currently know about your income and expenses.
Step 2: Estimate the unknowns until you have solid numbers.
Step 3: Adjust as reality unfolds.

If this isn't your strong suit, get help from someone who knows how to do it!

My number one business tool – a cash flow spreadsheet

Everyone who knows me well knows how much I love a spreadsheet. I set up my system on Excel in my early 20s and have used it ever since. No fancy or expensive tech needed, because I haven't found anything that works as well.

With every business I've worked in, the first thing I do is build a cash flow forecast. I track expected income and expenses for each week of the year and update it almost daily. I wouldn't have been able to do my job without it and it's been an essential tool for my role in finance.

- If you don't have a spreadsheet for this task, get one.
- If you don't know how to use a spreadsheet, find someone who does.

Please – Control your cash flow, or you'll end up with an empty bucket!

Pay Your Bills on Time, Every Time

A bad credit rating, repeated over time, will destroy trust with your suppliers and damage your reputation.

Pay bills on the due date.

End of.

One late bill, added to another late bill over time, will add up and before you know it you'll be drowning in debt, not knowing who to pay first. So, get into a regular monthly routine where everyone who is due to be paid, is paid.

At the end of each month, once all your bills have been entered into your accounting software or spreadsheet, you can add them up, split into the different payment terms and enter the figures due into your cash flow spreadsheet. Now you know well in advance what's due to go out and when.

All online banking will allow you to process payments in advance of the payment date; we usually do ours at the end of week three or the beginning of week four. Add them into the banking system, schedule for the last working day of the month and you're sorted!

Send a remittance advice (notice of what is being paid) to your supplier before payment date and everyone is happy.

You can now rest before the end of the month arrives, knowing everyone has been paid.

However, before you know it, a new month will have started, and it will be time to do it all again!

Be Honest with Everyone

I've worked with some wonderful customers and clients over the years, but the biggest bugbear of mine is lack of communication when it comes to paying their accounts.

When my team and I are sending out statements at the end of each month, followed by a polite reminder, followed by a telephone call, followed by a firmer 7-day warning letter and there's zero response, I tend to lose patience. It's at this point, after many attempts, that I'll send the account to our solicitors for chasing.

They will send a formal 7-day warning, after which time if there's still no response it will be sent to the local court and a CCJ (County Court Judgement) will be placed on their credit report. I absolutely hate doing this and it's really the last resort, but sometimes it's necessary for the protection and longevity of your own business.

A CCJ is immediately bad news for a business's credit ratings with other suppliers. If you can, avoid this at all costs by... you guessed it... paying your bills on time!

On the flipside, I've called customers after a statement and a follow-up has resulted in no payment and politely asked for the overdue account to be paid. Some people, because they're busy with other tasks, have simply forgotten and send the funds straightaway; others will explain that cash flow is a little tight, but they'll send something over by the end of the week or month.

This I don't mind. This I welcome. I appreciate some businesses are occasionally struggling with cash flow – maybe one of their customers has let them down. If I can see they have a good history and usually pay on time, albeit a little late on a few occasions, I'll make notes on the file, put a reminder in my diary and follow up with them the following week.

My point here is about communication. Talk to me, talk to your suppliers, let them know the situation! The last thing they want to do is lose you as a customer, so it's only in the most extreme cases where accounts are sent to court.

Sometimes it must be done though. A failure to take this action and not trigger this final stage can result in you being named on a creditors' list in liquidation papers when the customer has gone bust and you were too late.

The probability of you receiving anywhere near your outstanding amount is then virtually zero.

Don't Put Your Head in the Sand

This is the worst thing you can do.

"If I don't look at the amount we owe, it will go away."

"If I pretend it's not happening and just focus on getting the sales in it will be ok."

It won't!

Get it sorted, get the accounts up to date, get people paid and keep it that way!

There are only 12 financial cycles in a year and they pretty much all repeat the same.

Do it!

I've seen great businesses fold, not because they didn't have a good product or service, but because they didn't look after the finances. It always ends in misery.

Your finance person, whether they work with you full-time or part-time, employed or are contracted a few days a month, will be one of the key people on your team.

Building up trust with your finance person can take time. One of my old clients took about two years to trust me to have access to his bank account and pay his bills for him. I get it. It's their baby, their livelihood and I 'could' have run his account dry and run off into the sunset.

However, as a single mum of one, running my own business, the last thing I needed was a prison sentence for fraud and theft. Regardless of that, I would never ever do it – my morals, ethics and values would not allow it. He didn't know that though. But it happens, and it takes time to really trust a person, especially when they have access to your company money and everything you've been building up.

Finance people (bookkeepers, accountants, finance directors) are often under-valued members of the team. Some business owners think they don't even need one. But let me assure you, the right one will be worth their weight in gold!

Part 6

Lessons Learned

Introduction

We've reached a fitting point in this book where I can now summarise the biggest lessons I've learned over the past 32 years. I'm a firm believer that we never stop learning and so I look forward to the next teachings coming my way.

I've Quit Numerous Times

When I've felt that something is no longer working, I've quit. Not straightaway of course. I'll usually take some time to think things over, assess the situation, weigh up the pros and cons. Invariably though I've known when to move on and that process begins with quitting the things that were no longer right for me, were draining my energy or in severe cases being destructive to me and possibly others.

Brownies – They wanted me to become a fully-fledged member and wear their uniform. Not for me. I didn't go back. Even then I wasn't going to be told what to wear! I was seven!

Gymnastics – I broke my arm for the second time, falling off the bars. It damaged my confidence, and I was too scared to return. I quit. Regretfully on that occasion actually, although I didn't have the physique or natural skills to be a champion, so it was probably for the best anyway. My daughter and nieces are fabulous gymnasts, and my eldest niece is on the county team.

A-Levels – See my chapter on 'Bailing Out of Sixth Form'.

Family firm – I needed to spread my wings. This one took a few attempts, as it was deep-rooted with emotional connections. For me, having achieved success away from the family has been good and what I needed to do.

Marriage – We were both terribly unhappy. It's tragic and sad and caused a lot of hurt. It happens and you move on. You carry the scars, but you move on. We're both in new and happy relationships now and that's all you wish for each other.

Relationships – Toxic situations. Ones where they're bad for your health or ones that will never progress into meaningful ones, they're best to get out of.

Businesses – I've built, I've grown, and I've sold. Then moved on to the next challenge.

Jobs – When there's been no progression opportunities, or I've simply needed a new direction for personal growth. Quitting is ok – as long as you're not building up a huge history of short-term movement on your CV, as that can work against you and show you're not good at sticking at things.

Don't be afraid to quit, when it feels right... it usually is.

No One Can Take Away Your Skills

It doesn't matter if you lose your job, your home, or even your wealth, because the things you get to keep forever are the knowledge, skills and experience you've gained along the way.

They are yours. No one can take them away.

And if you ever need to start over?

You take with you your tenacity, your strength, your sense of humour (if you have one of course), your IT skills, your Microsoft knowledge, your qualifications… every asset you've built within yourself.

Here's a powerful question:

If you lost everything tomorrow and were left with nothing but the clothes on your back, could you find a way to earn a living, build a home, and make new connections?

I know I could.

Because I have:

- The ability to network. I know how to start conversations, ask for help, and build relationships.
- A strong work ethic, instilled in me by my parents. I can turn my hand to any task, no matter how small.
- The power of compounding. I understand that every small effort builds momentum. Every £1 earned, saved and invested eventually grows.
- The ability to give and receive kindness. I believe that helping others along the way creates a network of support when you need it most.

If you fear losing your wealth, job, home, car, or even friends, don't.

Instead, focus on building your personal assets.

Because your skills, knowledge and character are the most valuable investments you will ever make. And no matter what happens, they will always be yours.

Trust Your Instincts

Sometimes, the warning signs in life come at you loud and clear, screaming for attention. Other times, they're subtle whispers, nudging you gently in the background.

Either way, they are always there.

And yet, how often do we ignore them?

We stay in toxic relationships, tolerate unreliable friends, endure useless bosses.

Why?

Because we justify staying. We tell ourselves a story, convincing us that ignoring the signs is easier than facing the truth.

But here's the thing – there's always a reason behind that behaviour.

So, what's yours?

The real breakthrough comes when you dig deep and uncover the root cause of why you're stuck.

Because when you do, it usually opens up the path to a solution.

The battle between your heart and your head, between logic and instinct, between your brain and your gut, finally starts to make sense.

And that's when you know it's time to listen.

Don't Focus on the Competition

Just focus on what you are doing and aim to be the best at it. Every moment spent looking to your right, left, or behind you is time wasted, time that could be driving you and your business forward.

We all have the same 24 hours in a day. No one gets any more than anyone else. The difference is in how we use them, so make sure you are spending yours productively, investing in yourself and your future.

Be like a racehorse with blinkers on.

Think about it.

Does the horse worry about the horse next to it? No. It's blocked out. The only thing on its mind is running the race and crossing th finish line.

I've seen business owners become obsessed with what others are doing, stalking competitors across social media, waiting for the next announcement or product launch, only to copy it or try to outdo it.

What emotion do you think is driving that behaviour? Do you think it's positive? I don't. I think it's relentlessly negative and completely counterproductive.

Yes, it's important to stay informed about your peers in the marketplace, maybe even download their accounts at year-end to benchmark against your own. But that's something to do occasionally, not obsessively.

Your focus should be on you. On your business. On your creativity. Be unique.

Be the business your customers choose, for a reason. That's what will set you apart.

Confidence

I wasn't a confident child. I was shy, introverted and quietly spoken. I didn't naturally command attention or speak up in a crowd.

I believe we're all born confident. We come out into the world wanting to survive and make our mark. Then life happens, childhood happens, people influence us and erode that confidence or dent it.

But we can all build it back up again. Trust me, I've done it.

For me, confidence grew through experience, resilience, and pushing past challenges. Every difficulty I faced down, every setback I overcame, and every time I stepped outside my comfort zone onto (a metaphorical or real) stage, I became stronger. Small wins led to bigger ones, and before I knew it, I was leading teams, making decisions, and standing my ground in boardrooms.

Knowledge breeds confidence. The more I learned and prepared, the more assured I became, practising over and over again. I took action, despite my fears, because confidence isn't the absence of fear; it's moving forward in spite of it.

I learnt from my failures. Every mistake became a lesson, and every lesson made me more resilient. The more I practised, the better my speaking in public became.

Now, confidence is second nature to me, not because I never doubt myself (I do of course on occasion) but because I trust my ability to figure things out. I know I have a valid voice and that my opinions are valid. Not everyone may agree with me; they don't have to, and I don't mind that.

True confidence isn't about always knowing the answer; it's about believing you can find a way forward.

If you're not naturally confident, don't worry. It's a skill you build through action, perseverance and self-belief.

The more you challenge yourself, the more you grow, and then confidence will follow.

What Someone Else Thinks of You...

"What someone else thinks of you is none of your f*&^ing business."

WOW!

That might sound like just another self-help mantra, but this is one of the most liberating truths I've heard in my lifetime. It was on the first day on my hypnotherapy course in Southend, Essex, in April 2006. The tutor, Terence Watts, came out with it in his opening talk to our group of 18.

It has stayed with me ever since.

We live in a world full of noise.

Opinions, expectations and judgements are flying at us from every angle, ever more so in this era of social media. It's easy to slip into the trap of people-pleasing, basing decisions on how we think others will perceive us. Whether it's the way we dress, run our businesses, or the goals we chase, there's that constant inner voice asking, "But what will they think?"

Here's the reality.

You will never please everyone.

Someone will always have something to say. And if you let other people's opinions define your worth, you'll spend your life chasing approval that never lasts.

Your self-worth comes from within. It's rooted in how you see yourself, how you live your values, and how you show up for you. When you stop relying on others for validation, you stop living for their standards and start living by your own.

The more you build your own inner confidence without the struggle of pleasing others at the same time, the less their opinions matter. You begin making decisions based on what's right for your life, not what makes someone else comfortable.

And the greatest thing is that authenticity is magnetic.

The more you live and speak your truth, the more you attract people who respect and value the real you.

No pretending.

Just honest, aligned connections that actually matter.

The truth is, what someone else thinks of you doesn't impact your success, your happiness or your potential, unless you let it.

Focus on your goals, your growth, and your gut instinct. The rest? Let it go.

Trust yourself. Live authentically. The right people and the right results will follow.

Keep Getting Back Up Again

You're human. We all are.

Sometimes I think we forget that and assume we're all machines that can keep going, with the odd repair every now and again.

At some point an event or person is going to knock you sideways and on occasion down to ground (metaphorically speaking). It will dent any confidence you've built up; you'll question your decision-making, maybe lose friends, family or money, and life will be dark and dismal for a while.

What I know though is that you must, must, must, summon up the strength to get back up and on your feet again. It won't be easy; everyone may be telling you you're wrong, that maybe you're stupid, asking you how this could have happened?

Somewhere deep down in your core will be that fighting spirit, the one that's been with you from birth, the one that when the chips are down and the noise stops you can hear quietly to begin with and then louder and louder until you can ignore it no more.

That is what you need to nurture and build as big as possible.

It's time to stop being the victim. It's time to stop thinking negatively and it's time to get back up again.

Now, that all sounds quite simple, doesn't it?

I know that it isn't.

The one thing I'm most proud of over my past 'almost 50 years' on this planet (eek!) is asking for help and getting it when I really needed it. This is not something that has come easy to me. I'm the kinda girl who likes to do stuff for herself, has a fiercely independent streak and is stubborn (don't tell my partner I admitted to that one!).

So, finding the humility to ask for help when I've been on the floor has been the making of me. I sought out a therapist after my daughter was born, feeling like I was the worst mother on the planet, which was odd to me, because before she was born, I was planning on being Earth Mother Reincarnated. Anyway, therapy did the trick big time when I was really struggling. I was told to get back to work a couple of days a week and to put my daughter into a nursery.

That was all rather a bombshell to me at the time, but it was the permission I needed to do just that, to not feel guilty about it, and to learn that I was not wired the same as everyone else. What a relief!

My daughter is still best friends with the little girl she met at nursery, and they now travel the world together. Her mum is one of my closest friends. Not only did both of us make long-lasting friendships, my daughter gained valuable social skills from an early age that have set up her for life. From a challenging situation some life-changing events occurred. I'd say that's a win-win, wouldn't you?

So, the process of 'Getting Back Up Again' can in fact be a long and very winding road.

The important thing is that you do it and every day you work towards staying up, looking after yourself and moving forward.

Moving On Is Ok

If you're not moving forward, you're either going backwards or stagnating, and neither of those are good options.

Yet, for some reason, society often makes us feel like moving on is a form of quitting, as if letting go of something means failure. But that couldn't be further from the truth. Moving on isn't about giving up, it's about growing.

Think about it. How can you evolve, improve, or reach new heights, if you never allow yourself to change course? Life isn't meant to be static.

Businesses pivot. Careers shift. People grow.

And the ones who achieve the most success are those who embrace the process of moving on when the time is right.

One of the hardest things to do is to let go of something you once loved or invested time in. A business you built, a job you once thrived in, a relationship that was once fulfilling. But just because something was right for you at one point doesn't mean it always will be.

Holding onto something out of habit, fear, or a sense of obligation, isn't noble, it's limiting. Staying in a job you hate, running a business that no longer excites you, or maintaining a friendship that drains you, doesn't serve anyone, least of all yourself.

Moving on doesn't mean forgetting the past. It doesn't mean what you had wasn't valuable. It simply means you're ready for the next chapter.

Every success story includes moments when someone had to move on. Entrepreneurs sell businesses to start new ones. Athletes retire and move into coaching or business. People relocate for new opportunities. These transitions aren't failures, they're stepping-stones to something even greater.

Imagine if Apple had never moved on from the iPod, or if top athletes clung to their playing careers long past their peak. Moving on is necessary for growth, reinvention and success.

Sometimes, the hardest part of moving on is the fear of what others will think. Will they say you gave up? Will they question your decision? Maybe. But what matters more is what you think.

Give yourself permission to change. To walk away from something that no longer fits. To pursue a new direction. To admit that what once worked for you no longer does. That's not failure, that's wisdom.

If you've been feeling stuck, frustrated or unfulfilled, ask yourself — is it time to move on?

Trust your instincts. Change is uncomfortable, but so is staying in the wrong place for too long. Moving on is ok. In fact, it's essential.

Because the best things in life aren't behind you. They're ahead.

No One Will Talk About Your Ironing at Your Funeral!

My friend and I often chew the fat about motherhood, partners, kids, and life in general. It's such a relief to have someone to talk to, a safe space where we can share whatever is on our minds without fear of judgement or criticism.

One day, a few years ago, we were chatting about household tasks, and one of us (I can't quite remember who!) was gearing up to tackle the mountain of ironing that had built up at home. Thinking back, it would most probably have been me! Domestic duties have never been my strongest priority. We can't be good at everything hey?

Anyway, I'd recently been to a funeral, and as we were talking, I said something along the lines of, "No one's going to remember how well you did the ironing or how clean your house was, at your funeral, are they?"

And, well, think about it, they won't! At every funeral I've attended, no one has ever said, "She always kept the house spotless" or "Wasn't she great at tackling that mountain of ironing?" Nobody has reminisced about how pristine the house looked or how perfectly pressed the shirts were. And let's be real, I've never heard anyone praise the completion of domestic tasks that often feel like such an uphill battle.

This got me thinking. Sometimes, we need to pause and consider what really matters in life. We spend so much energy worrying about day-to-day pressures, trying to perform, achieve, and sometimes outdo everyone else. But is that really what is important?

Take a moment to stop. Reflect. Instead of stressing over the mundane, think about how you want to be remembered. What would you like people to say about you at your funeral? Now, I know that is a bit morbid, but this kind of thinking helps you gain perspective on what really counts. Work backwards from those conversations you'd want to hear. What would be said about the way you lived, loved, and impacted those around you? Once you have that clear, you'll realise that the tasks you're caught up in today might not be the ones that matter most in the grand scheme of things.

So, take a deep breath, let go of the little things, and focus on what truly leaves a lasting impression: your actions, your kindness, your legacy.

The ironing can wait!

Treat Your Goals Like Car Journeys

"I'm working really hard! But it just feels like I'm going round in circles."

Sounds familiar? I hear it all the time, business owners working their backsides off day in, day out, only to end up in the same place at the end of the year, or worse, falling behind.

Now, imagine your business is like driving a car. Where is your Satnav programmed to take you? Are you moving forward, or just circling the M25, burning fuel, using energy, but never really getting anywhere?

On the flipside, let's say you've planned your journey. You're heading from London to Edinburgh, and you're already halfway there. Fantastic! You know where you're going, and every mile brings you closer.

The first important step, before you even set off, is knowing your destination!

If you've got a meeting, you check the address, figure out the time you need to be there, and work backwards. "I need to be in Birmingham at 4pm tomorrow, so I should leave at 1pm to allow for traffic."

Why should your business be any different?

Start with your end destination in mind, whether that is the end of the month, the quarter, or the year. Then plot the most efficient route to get there. Along the way, you'll need to refuel, take breaks, and maybe adjust for unexpected diversions (or in business terms, deal with cash flow issues, supplier hiccups, or staffing problems).

If you don't plan ahead, you're performing the business equivalent of jumping in a camper van on a sunny afternoon and just seeing where the road takes you. That's great for a road trip, not so great when your business and livelihood are at stake.

My business road map to success

- **Set the destination:** Define your business goal clearly. Where do you want to be by a specific time?

- **Plan your route:** Work out the steps to get there. There's always more than one way!

- **Check your timings:** Set realistic deadlines to keep yourself accountable.

- **Be adaptable:** Expect roadblocks and detours. The route may change, but the goal stays the same.

- **Keep checking your direction:** Regularly review your progress, to stay on track.

- **Arrive at your destination:** Celebrate the achievement before setting your next goal!

So, think about it, would you ever set off on a journey without knowing where you were heading? No! Then don't do it in business either.

Get your map out and plan your route. You'll get there faster, with less stress, and a whole lot more success.

Drive, Walk, Shower!

Have you ever been stuck, staring at a screen, trying to force a breakthrough, only to have your best idea hit you while you're driving, walking, or taking a shower?

Funny that... me too!

It's almost as if the harder you try to think of a solution, the further away it gets. But the moment you step back and do something completely unrelated to work, your brain suddenly fires up with creativity and clarity. It feels like magic, but in reality, it's science.

Our brains operate in two ways – logical and creative. When we're glued to a screen or buried in a spreadsheet, we're operating in focused mode. This is great for getting things done, but not so great for creativity.

To generate fresh ideas and get those creative channels unblocked, you need to disengage from the logical side of your brain and allow the creative side to take over. The best way to do this? Step away.

Some of my best ideas have come to me when I'm either driving, walking, or showering. Why? I often wondered this, but I've learnt over the years that it's because these activities put us in a state of relaxed awareness, where our minds can wander freely.

Driving – Ever found yourself on autopilot during a familiar drive, only to suddenly have a flash of insight? That's because your brain isn't overloaded with stuff and with logical thinking. It has space to process thoughts in the background.

Walking – Moving through nature (which is my favourite pastime outside of work) or even just pacing around at home can stimulate new ideas.

Showering – The warm water, the rhythmic sounds and the solitude, create the perfect conditions for creativity to strike.

In today's always-on world, we're conditioned to believe that productivity comes from grinding through tasks. But true innovation doesn't happen when you're forcing it. It happens when your brain has the space to connect the dots in ways you wouldn't expect.

So, if you're stuck in a creative rut or can't seem to solve a problem, stop forcing it. Take a drive, go for a walk, or jump in the shower. Let your subconscious mind take over.

Don't stress if a big idea doesn't hit immediately. Just enjoy the break, let your mind breathe, and before you know it, the cogs will start whirring again.

The trick is to trust the process.

Keep Making Positive Plans

It's difficult sometimes when life throws you a curve ball or puts distractions in your way. You can get thrown off course, feel down or depressed and wonder what the whole point of it all is.

I always do my best and aim to keep myself moving forward. This I believe is the foundation of growth, success and personal development. But how do we ensure that we're consistently moving forward in the right direction? The answer lies in your plans… your positive plans.

Your subconscious brain is a remarkable tool and ultimately it works to keep you safe and alive. It doesn't process information logically; instead, it picks up on the signals you send it. Think of it like a GPS. It doesn't question your destination; it just gets to work following the coordinates you give it. So, if you're constantly focusing on negative outcomes, fears and doubts, that's the direction your subconscious will move you toward.

When you're always anticipating obstacles, fearing the next step, or dreading that leap of faith, guess what happens? You'll start to notice more roadblocks, more resistance, and more hesitation. Your subconscious will work overtime to confirm those fears, making it even harder to take action. Negative thinking creates a cycle that holds you back. This is why it's crucial to consciously choose positive plans and set your sights on what you truly want to achieve.

The good news? Your subconscious is just as willing to follow a positive direction if you allow it to. The more you focus on what you want, rather than what you fear, the more your mind will work to make that happen. This is where the magic happens! When you make a habit of planning positively, you begin to break free from the chains of self-doubt and fear.

Ask yourself these questions to get started:

"What do I *want* to happen?"

Focus on your desired outcome. Whether it's growing your business, hitting a new revenue target, or finding a better work-life balance, make sure you're clear about what success looks like for you.

"What do I believe *will* happen when I take action?"

Don't leave room for doubt. Confidence comes from knowing that action leads to results. When you believe in the positive impact of your efforts, you align your subconscious to work in your favour. Start expecting success, and your actions will follow.

"How will it *look* and *feel* when I've achieved it?"

This is where you begin to visualise your success. Imagine yourself crossing that finish line. How do you feel? How does your success change your life or your business? Visualisation is an incredibly powerful tool because it sets your brain into feeling like it's already happening, which boosts your motivation to take action.

Thinking positively is one thing but planning positively is where the magic happens. It's essential to write down your goals, create a timeline, and outline your next steps. Putting your intentions on paper strengthens them and makes them real. Keep your plans clear and focused on the outcome you desire. For example, instead of writing, "I don't want to fail," reframe this as, "I will successfully launch this new product by the end of the month". This shifts the focus from fear to accomplishment, aligning your plans with your positive intentions.

Now that we have some positive plans in mind, it's time to get them out of your head and onto paper.

This may sound a bit old-fashioned in today's digital age, but bear with me. The act of writing things down with a pen and paper is far more powerful than you might think. It engages different parts of the brain, and here's why. When you type on a computer, you're typically engaging the left side of your brain, the logical, analytical part. But writing by hand taps into the right side, the creative, problem-solving part of your brain. This is a key reason why I always turn to pen and paper when I need to brainstorm, problem-solve, or release pent-up ideas. It's a surprisingly simple but incredibly effective tool.

I encourage you to find yourself the loveliest notebook you can and pair it with a quality pen (no cheap ballpoints, please!).

Sit down and let your thoughts flow. Use this time to let your creativity take the lead and map out your plans in detail.

Once you have your ideas flowing and organised, you can transfer them to a computer, but for pure creative brainstorming, pen and paper are my winning combination.

In fact, this book you're reading started in a coffee shop, with just an A5 notebook and a pen. Those early scribbled ideas have become the foundation for everything that has followed. It took time to build, but without that initial step, I wouldn't have had a structure to grow from or a clear sense of where my story was headed.

So, grab that notebook, let your thoughts spill onto the page, and watch how the act of writing things down can transform your plans and your mindset.

Tunnel Vision for the Win

There comes a time in business, and in life, when the only way forward is right straight through the middle. You've taken a hit, whether financial, emotional, or both, and everywhere you turn, the noise is deafening. Doubters, critics, and even your own inner voice, tell you it's over. The weight of failure feels unbearable.

I know that feeling. I have lived it. After an event that left me emotionally drained and financially rocked, the voices of negativity were relentless. Some were external, people who claimed they were "only trying to help," offering their opinions on what I should or shouldn't have done. Others were internal, the ones whispering self-doubt in the quiet moments. It would have been easy to let it consume me, to spiral into over-analysis and regret.

But I chose a different path.

When everything feels like it's caving in, the first step is to shut out the negativity. That doesn't mean ignoring reality, it means filtering out the distractions that do nothing but hold you back.

Think about a tunnel. It's dark. It's narrow. But there is one thing that remains constant, the light at the end. That's where your focus needs to be. The voices, the setbacks, the doubts? They're just echoes in the tunnel walls. Let them exist, but don't let them dictate your direction.

In moments of difficulty, your vision must be sharper than ever. It's easy to get lost in analysing every mistake, overthinking every move, or trying to respond to every critic. But none of that will help you get back on your feet. The only thing that matters is moving forward.

This is where tunnel vision becomes a survival tool. You don't look left, you don't look right, and you certainly don't look back. You focus on the one thing that will get you out of the situation, your goal. Whether it's rebuilding your business, regaining financial stability, or reclaiming your confidence, keep your eyes locked on that target.

There are times when being open-minded, adaptable, and aware of your surroundings, is beneficial. But when you're at rock bottom, tunnel vision is the key to survival. It simplifies the chaos, strips away the distractions, and forces you to concentrate on what really matters.

Some may call it stubbornness. I call it determination.

When I was down, I made a choice. I would not be defined by that moment. I refused to let the weight of negativity dictate my future. Instead, I locked my eyes on the goal, shut out everything that didn't serve it, and took step after step until I was out of the tunnel.

And when I emerged, I was stronger, wiser, and more focused than ever. It was actually the making of me!

So, if you find yourself lost, overwhelmed, or drowning in doubt, remember this:

Tunnel vision for the win. Focus on the light. Keep moving forward. And never let the noise pull you off course.

Know What You Sell and to Who

This might seem like an obvious statement, but do you really know what you sell?

If I asked you to describe your product or service in one sentence, could you do it? Not in a long-winded, jargon-filled way, but in a simple, clear and compelling statement?

Nailing this is the first step in building a strong business foundation. When you truly understand your core offering, everything else falls into place. Your ideal customer becomes clearer, your marketing more effective, and your sales process more streamlined.

At first glance, this might seem straightforward. If you're a florist, you sell flowers. If you're an accountant, you sell financial services. But dig a little deeper, and you'll find it's about much more than that.

Florists don't just sell flowers, they sell emotions, celebrations, and moments of appreciation.

Accountants don't just do taxes, they provide peace of mind, financial security, and business growth.

Gyms don't just offer workouts, they sell confidence, health, and lifestyle transformation.

Understanding the real value behind what you sell changes how you position your business. It's not just about the product or service, it's about the outcome and impact you create for your customers.

The best businesses can sum up what they do in one clear, simple sentence. If your answer is overly complicated, you risk confusing potential customers and missing opportunities.

When you simplify your message, your business becomes more recognisable, memorable, and marketable.

Once you've nailed what you sell, the next step is understanding who needs it. Your ideal customers should be easy to identify when you're clear on your offering.

Ask yourself:

- Who benefits most from what I sell?
- What problems do they have that I solve?
- Why would they choose me over someone else?

The clearer you are on your ideal customer, the easier it is to craft marketing messages that resonate with them.

If you can't clearly explain what you sell, your customers won't understand it either. And if they don't understand it, they won't buy it.

So, take a step back and define it. Keep it simple, focus on the value, and make sure it's crystal clear.

Because when you know what you sell, you can sell it with confidence and that's when business truly takes off.

Know Where to Communicate

Once you're clear on what you sell and who your customers are, the next step is knowing where to reach them. Sounds simple, but many businesses waste time and money shouting into the void, posting in the wrong places and hoping someone bites. I won't be going into in-depth marketing strategies here; I merely want to share my basic tips.

Start by truly understanding your ideal customer:

- Who are they?
- Where do they hang out, online and offline?
- How do they consume content?
- What problems are they trying to solve?

If you're targeting an older business owner, TikTok probably isn't your winner. But LinkedIn, email, trade magazines or networking events? Absolutely.

If you're speaking to Gen Z, an email newsletter won't land like a well-timed TikTok or Insta reel.

The goal is to meet people where they already are, not where it's convenient for you.

Communication channels that work

Social media

- **LinkedIn** – B2B, professional services, decision-makers. I love this one!

- **Facebook** – Local audiences, community-driven marketing. For the right audience, absolutely!

- **Instagram/TikTok** – Younger, lifestyle-focused consumers. I use Instagram but not to its full potential yet; TikTok I wouldn't know how to use!

- **X (Twitter)** – Thought leadership, trends, quick engagement. Not for me but for you, maybe!

Email marketing

Great for both B2B and B2C when done right. I use Mailchimp and LeadConnector, great for looking at performance and engagement statistics after you've sent emails.

Networking & events

- Gold for building real relationships. I love networking!
- Works brilliantly with decision-makers, industry pros, and high-value clients.

Traditional media

Expensive, but strategic print/radio/direct mail can work if your audience isn't digital-first.

Content & SEO

Blogs, podcasts and videos position you as the expert in your field. I love these!

Don't market where it's easiest; market where it's effective. Your next customer is already listening somewhere. Make sure it's to you.

Rapport, Trust & Integrity

People buy from people. If they don't like you, you have no chance. If they don't trust you, even less. Remember, you won't gel with everyone so don't over-try if it's really not happening.

Business success isn't just about having the best product, it's about relationships. The greatest deal means nothing if customers don't feel comfortable with you. That's why rapport, trust and integrity are key, and relationships are fundamental.

Rapport

Rapport is about connection, finding common ground through shared interests, values, or even humour. It's not about faking it but creating genuine relationships by:

- Showing real interest in their business and challenges.
- Subtly mirroring their communication style.
- Finding shared experiences to build a bond.

If you can go for a coffee and end up chatting about what you did at the weekend on a mutual level then you're on to a winner. Don't worry about selling anything at this stage. You just want to build a connection. It may not be the person directly in front of you who will end up buying either, but one of their contacts they've passed your number on to.

Trust

Rapport gets the conversation started and trust leads you closer to being the go-to person for your product or service. Customers need confidence that you'll deliver. Trust is earned through:

- Reliability – Do what you say you will, every time.
- Honesty – If something isn't right for them, say so. Own up to mistakes.
- Listening – Understanding their needs proves you're there to help, not just sell.

A good friend of mine said we're born with one mouth and two ears for a reason. You're supposed to listen more than you talk!

Integrity

Integrity ties it all together. It's about doing the right thing, even when no one's watching. It means:

- Being transparent in all dealings.
- Treating people with respect.
- Owning mistakes and making them right.

Want people to buy from and recommend you? Be the kind of person you'd want to do business with.

Build real connections, earn trust, and operate with integrity, then success will follow.

Sales Funnel

Let's be honest, no one wakes up one morning, stumbles across your business, and shouts, "Take my money!" That's not how buying decisions work.

Whether you realise it or not, every customer goes on a bit of a journey before they buy from you. And that journey? That's your sales funnel.

Don't let the jargon put you off, this isn't just marketing fluff. It's about understanding how people move from "Who are you?" to "Where have you been all my life?"

A good sales funnel is like a road map. It takes someone from curiosity to commitment, step by step. And if you get it right, it doesn't just land you the first sale, it builds trust, loyalty and repeat business. That's where the real value is.

Think about your own buying habits. You probably don't jump into big decisions without a bit of research, a recommendation, or at least a gut check. Your customers are no different. They need to see you, hear from you, get a feel for what you do and then, when the time's right, they'll be ready to buy. But if you're not guiding them through that process, you risk losing them somewhere along the way.

The key is intention. Too many businesses throw out content, offers or social posts and just hope for the best. But when you know what stage your audience is at – just browsing, weighing up their options, or ready to buy – you can speak to them in a way that actually lands.

The goal isn't just to get a quick win. It's to create such a solid, value-packed journey that people want to come back, refer you, and become genuine fans of your business.

That's what a good sales funnel does. It builds trust, not just transactions.

Make It Easy for People to Say Yes

In business, success isn't just about having a brilliant product or service, it's about making it ridiculously easy for people to say yes. The faster someone can make a decision, the faster you see results.

Most businesses unknowingly make it harder than it needs to be. Confusing pricing, vague offers, broken links, too many hoops to jump through — it's like setting up your own obstacle course. I don't know about you, but I'll lose interest and leave a website if it's too complicated to buy or even just reach the next level.

If you want more sales, partnerships or opportunities, your job is to clear the path. That means making everything feel simple, obvious and completely risk-free.

Start with clarity. If people can't understand what you're offering in a few seconds, they'll scroll past or click away. Keep your message simple, ditch the jargon, and be direct about the value you bring. If someone has to ask, "What exactly do you do?" you've already lost them.

Next, reduce the effort needed to take action. Whether it's booking a call, placing an order or getting in touch, make it seamless. Too many steps and people will give up. Make it one-click easy.

Then, kill the fear. Everyone's a bit sceptical, we're all being pitched to daily. So back yourself up. Use testimonials. Share real results. Offer guarantees or flexible cancellation policies. Confidence is contagious when people can see you've delivered before.

And don't forget the golden rule: make the next step obvious. If someone's ready to take action, don't leave them guessing. Tell them exactly what to do and make it effortless, whether that's clicking a link, choosing a package, or giving you a call.

The goal is simple – make working with you the easiest decision they'll make that day.

When saying yes feels like the natural choice, you don't have to push people, they'll step forward on their own. That's how you move from interest to income.

No Hard Sell

Having grown up in the double-glazing industry I am fully accustomed to the 'hard sell' approach, and it still bugs the hell out of me. It's an instant sale killer in my book.

Listen to your potential customer, answer their questions, provide them with all the opportunities your service or product has to offer, at a price that is fair and reasonable and then... leave them to decide for themselves.

If you've built up rapport, trust and integrity during this process there is little else you can do. Trying to force a sale will backfire, in my experience.

"You Can Take My Offer and Accept It or Light the Fire With It!"

My dad's sales pitch was great.

The double-glazing industry in the 80s and 90s was brutal; it probably still is, I don't know. Back then it was very aggressive. The hard sell was usual practice and some stories we heard would appear on crime channels now.

There were discounts for having a board up in your garden; there were late night calls to the 'Manager' to get an extra 20% off; there were appointments that lasted in people's home for around four hours. In the end the sales rep would probably get thrown out. It was awful.

Dad had a different approach.

He would spend a maximum of an hour in someone's home. He would work out the quotation, usually at the same time, give the person the price, saying it was his best price straightaway and then invite the customer to accept it or be free to light the fire with it!

Sounds harsh when written out like this I know, but with his charismatic charm and friendly nature the point he was trying to make was that there would be no hard sell, no promise of 'discounts' that were never there in the first place, and that he wouldn't be chasing them up on the telephone every day for the next week until they signed the contract.

In addition to this he offered a policy of no deposit and you paid in full when the job was complete and you were happy.

Make it easy for people to say yes!

Upsell

Upselling increases revenue, yes, but adding real value for the customer? That's a game-changer!

Too many businesses see upselling as a simple way to make more money. They focus on squeezing a little extra out of each sale, pushing add-ons, or convincing customers to upgrade for the sake of it. But the best kind of upselling isn't about selling more, it's about solving more.

When you take a customer's initial enquiry and elevate it to a level they didn't even realise they needed, you're not just increasing your revenue, you're increasing their satisfaction. And that's where the magic happens.

Think about it — customers come to you with a problem. They might think they know what they need, but often they don't have the full picture. They only see the immediate issue in front of them. Your job, as an expert in your field, is to guide them toward a solution that works best for them, not just for now, but in the long run.

Imagine a customer walks into a car dealership looking for a basic model. They want something functional, a car that gets them from A to B. But through conversation, you realise they do a lot of long-distance travel. They've got kids. They need safety, comfort, and fuel efficiency. By guiding them towards a better-suited option, not just a more expensive one, that genuinely meets their needs, you've not only made a bigger sale, you've created a loyal customer.

And loyalty is priceless.

When people feel like you truly understand them, when they believe you're looking out for their best interests rather than just your own bottom line, they trust you. And trust leads to repeat business, long-term relationships and, most importantly, referrals.

A happy customer doesn't just come back; they tell everyone they know. They become your biggest fan, your loudest cheerleader, and your most valuable marketing asset. Word-of-mouth is still one of the most powerful drivers of business growth, and it starts with how well you serve the people already in front of you.

So, how do you do this effectively?

Listen first, sell second

Understand the customer's real needs, not just what they think they need. Ask the right questions, dig deeper, and uncover the bigger picture.

Educate, don't push

Show them the value in upgrading, expanding or enhancing their purchase. Help them see why it's the right choice, not just a more expensive one.

Solve problems, don't just sell products

Customers aren't looking for items or services, they're looking for solutions. If you can provide those, they'll come back to you every time.

At the end of the day, great businesses aren't built on quick sales. They're built on relationships, trust, and adding genuine value. Upselling isn't about taking more; it's about giving more. And when you do that, the revenue follows naturally.

Because when customers feel understood and looked after, they don't just buy, they believe. And that's what turns a one-time sale into a lifetime of loyalty.

Work/Life Balance

Success in business means nothing if it comes at the cost of your well-being or the relationships that matter most. This is so important. I keep a spreadsheet with a column for every area of my life, business and personal, and make sure I have done something in each of the areas every month.

Work/life balance isn't just about switching off at a certain time, it's about making sure that the energy and effort you put into work is matched by what you put into home life. Just like in business, a strong, supportive team at home makes all the difference. I'm pleased to say I have achieved this now. Of course, there are busy periods and times when I'm away working but on the whole my weekends and evenings are my own to spend with my family.

At work, you know the value of collaboration, communication, and having each other's backs. The same principles apply at home. Whether it's a partner, family, or close friends, you need people around you who uplift, support, and share the load. And just as you delegate tasks in business, don't be afraid to ask for help or offer it in return. A thriving home life isn't built by one person, it's a team effort. My partner and I both work, we share the tasks at home and cover each other when the other one needs to work.

Taking time out is just as important. You wouldn't run a business without strategic planning, and the same goes for personal time. Prioritise moments that recharge you, whether that's a quiet evening, a weekend getaway, or simply being present with loved ones.

Work hard, yes. Chase your goals, absolutely.

But remember, true success isn't just about what you achieve, it's about who you share it with and how you show up for them.

You'll Know When You're on the Right Path

It starts as a spark, an idea, a curiosity, a thought that won't quite let go. At first, it's just an exploration, a "What if?" moment. Then, almost before you realise it, that spark turns into an unstoppable energy, consuming your thoughts every waking hour. And those waking hours? They'll get longer. Because, let's be honest, things don't get done while you're sleeping, and there's a hell of a lot that needs doing!

It becomes the first thing on your mind when you wake up and the last thing before you fall asleep. Momentum kicks in. The snowball starts rolling, and suddenly you're struggling to keep up with the pace, even with all your energy and drive. Things aren't happening fast enough for your liking, but they are happening.

If you've ever questioned what your 'thing' is, your purpose, your reason for being, I can't tell you exactly what it is, you'll need to figure that one out yourself, but when you do find it, this is what will happen.

When everything starts aligning, when the excitement is

relentless, when you can't not do it… you're on the right path. Doors will open effortlessly. The right people will 'magically' appear just at the right moment. Opportunities will fall into place like they were waiting for you to show up. This isn't just theory. It's what's been happening to me as I finish writing this book at the start of 2025.

Everything I've worked on for the last 30 years, every job, every challenge, every late night and early morning, is coming together in ways I never even imagined. And that's how I know I'm exactly where I'm meant to be.

Trust the process. When you're on the right path, you'll feel it. And once you do, there's no turning back!

Celebrate Your Wins

Running a business isn't just about the hard work, the late nights, or the constant problem-solving. It's also about the wins, the milestones, the breakthroughs, and the moments of success that make the journey worthwhile.

Yet so many business owners overlook this part. They tell themselves, "I'll celebrate when I reach the next big goal," or "I can't afford to splash out right now". But here's the thing – if you don't take time to celebrate your wins, what's the point of all the effort?

Yes, cash flow might still be tight in your first year as a start-up. Yes, you might feel guilty spending money when you've been running on a budget. But celebrating success isn't about extravagance, it's about acknowledging progress.

Success, no matter how small, should be marked in some way. It reinforces the idea that you're moving forward, achieving what you set out to do, and creating a life that you can enjoy.

It doesn't have to be grand. It could be:

- Fish and chips for the team on a Friday after a productive week.
- A dinner out with your other half after landing a new contract.

Or if you want to go all out:

- A luxury holiday or first-class flight after smashing a major goal.
- A full-blown marquee event to celebrate a decade in business.

The scale of the celebration doesn't matter; it's about taking a moment to reflect, appreciate and enjoy the journey.

One of the best things about celebrating your wins is that it gives you memories to look back on. Take photos, write it down, document it in some way. In five or ten years, you'll be grateful you did. You'll be able to see how far you've come, and those moments will fuel you through the next stage of your journey.

I've been fortunate to celebrate success in incredible ways – dining in some of the best restaurants in the world, flying on a private jet, staying in luxurious hotels, and experiencing the first-class lifestyle. These moments weren't just about indulgence; they were about recognising achievements, marking progress, and allowing myself to enjoy the rewards of my hard work.

At the end of the day, running your own business isn't just about survival, it's about building a life you love. So, when you achieve something, big or small, don't brush past it.

Take a moment. Celebrate. Treat yourself. You've earned it.

Enjoy the Adventure!

Business isn't just about hitting targets and making profits; it should be an adventure. One that's often filled with twists, turns and unexpected detours. Some days, you'll feel on top of the world, making sales, building teams, and seeing your vision come to life. Other days, you'll wonder why you ever started. That's the nature of the ride.

But here's the thing – half the fun is in figuring it all out. Every challenge you face is an opportunity to grow, every setback a lesson, and every success a milestone that proves you're capable of more than you ever imagined. You'll develop resilience, sharpen your instincts, and learn what truly matters, not just in business, but in life.

And when you come out the other side of a tough situation, don't just move on to the next goal. Take a moment. Look back. Appreciate the process. The grit it took to push through, and the lessons you gained along the way. The toughest moments often turn out to be the ones that shaped you the most.

So, embrace the chaos, the uncertainty, the unexpected challenges. Enjoy the adventure of building something meaningful.

Because in the end, success isn't just about where you land, it's about how you got there and the person you became along the way.

Part 7

What Next for Me?

Introduction

What next indeed?

The biggest thing about getting older and reaching middle-age is the notion of mortality creeping up on me. Every time I think of that I just say to myself, "But I'm nowhere near done yet!"

This propels me to keep learning, keep achieving and keep driving forward. There is still much to do.

As I complete the writing of this book in spring 2025 it gives me a chance to reflect on where I've come from and what the road ahead looks like.

I can't see all the way of course, and I love not knowing exactly where it will lead.

But what I do know is that I'm definitely nowhere near done and there are still exciting adventures to come.

Finding Love Take #2

I could honestly write a whole book on the dating scene post-divorce because it's an absolute frickin' minefield! Maybe one day I will. For now, I'll stick to my story!

When I got married, quite young some would say at 22, I took the view that if things didn't work out for whatever reason, we'd get divorced and both move on with new people.

Just. Like. That.

Oh, how I love my younger self's outlook on the world, so innocent and simple!!

Let me tell you, there is very little 'just like that' in the whole process, believe me.

Dating as a single parent, 15–20 years on from when you did it first time round is a completely different kettle of humbugs.

One evening on a first date, the guy sat across from me at dinner texting his ex-girlfriend, liaising the childcare arrangements for the following day. I wouldn't usually mind, I'm a parent myself and you have to deal with this kind of thing when needed but it carried on for ages. I sat there like a lemon, refusing to get my own phone out in protest. Suffice to say, there was no second date.

Another time the guy lied about his height. I'm quite short at 5'2" but I towered over him. No second date either. It wasn't that he was short that bothered me, it was that he'd lied!

The thing with online dating is that you can get along perfectly well with someone over Messenger and then the day you meet in person I would know within 10 seconds that they weren't right. I would then have to go through the uncomfortable drinks and make my excuses, or worse dinner if I'd judged it completely wrong in advance.

Then in 2018, after deciding I was not in fact cut out for the convent or becoming a nun I decided to try again. This time I made my choices more specific. I knew who I was looking for and wasn't going to settle for less.

Keith and I began messaging in the autumn of 2018 and after a week of 'all day, everyday' messages, the kind that make your heart leap when the phone buzzes, we eventually agreed to meet. I prayed that he was going to be as nice in person as he was on the phone and thank God, this time I wasn't disappointed. We met in Stamford and spent a wonderful four hours together. I only left because I had to collect my daughter from school. We've been together ever since.

I won't lie that's it been all sunshine and roses. Second time round is difficult. Scars exist, emotional triggers flag up on occasion, and there are children involved whose emotional well-being is as important as our own. But you find a way of working through things and manage the difficulties as they arise, because at the end of the day you've chosen to be together. Not because you need to but because you want to and that's all that matters now.

We both love the new life we've built together and the new home we now share. It's been a ride and a half getting here but I wouldn't change a thing. It all goes into the life bucket of experiences.

My Passions

My journey in business has been shaped by a deep commitment to building strong teams, empowering people, and driving financial success. I've realised through the process of writing this book that at the heart of everything I do are four key passions:

Business – Building sustainable success

I believe in the power of well-structured, financially strong businesses. A thriving business isn't just about making a profit; it's about resilience, adaptability, and long-term sustainability. Success comes from having the right foundations in place, from strong financial management to an engaged and motivated team.

Having spent years working with SMEs across different industries, I've seen first-hand the challenges business owners face, whether it's managing cash flow, scaling effectively, or navigating economic uncertainties. My passion has been helping businesses overcome these hurdles by providing the right strategies, connections and financial insights to ensure they don't just survive but thrive.

People – The heart of every business

A business is only as strong as its people. Whether it's a small startup or an established company, the key to long-term success lies in attracting, developing and retaining the right talent. I'm passionate about fostering strong leadership, creating a culture of collaboration, and ensuring that people feel valued, supported, and empowered to reach their full potential.

Beyond employees, I believe in the power of strong business networks. The right connections can open doors, provide fresh perspectives, and lead to incredible opportunities. That's why I'm committed to bringing people together, whether it's through mentorship, business partnerships, or supporting entrepreneurs in their journeys.

UK SME community – Strengthening the backbone of our economy

Small and Medium Enterprises are the driving force behind the UK economy, yet they often struggle with access to resources, financial support, and a clear voice in government policies. Having worked with SMEs for decades, I understand the frustrations and roadblocks they face, from navigating complex regulations to securing the right funding and support.

I'm dedicated to supporting this community, ensuring they have a stronger voice in shaping the policies that impact them.

Supporting the younger generation with their entrepreneurial journeys

The future of business lies in the hands of young entrepreneurs, and I love to help equip them with the knowledge, confidence and resources they need to succeed. Starting a business can be daunting, especially for those who lack experience or financial backing. That's why mentorship, guidance and real-world insights are so valuable.

I want to inspire the next generation to dream big, take smart risks, and build businesses that make a difference. Whether it's through sharing my own experiences, providing financial literacy education, or connecting young entrepreneurs with the right people, I'm committed to helping them navigate the challenges of business ownership.

Supporting the younger generation isn't just about the businesses they'll create, it's about fostering a mindset of resilience, problem-solving and innovation that will serve them throughout their careers.

Bringing it all together

These four passions drive me every day. Whether it's supporting SMEs, strengthening business teams, or guiding the next generation of entrepreneurs, my mission is to, in my own small way, build a stronger, more resilient business community. By combining financial expertise with a people-first approach.

Writing This Book

Writing this book has been such joy!

Both rewarding and fulfilling, I've achieved a long-held ambition of getting my stories down into print. It's not every day you sit down to reflect on over three decades of business and personal growth, and it's been a fantastic project to work on. I'm so thrilled to be finally sharing it with you.

As I poured my thoughts onto the page, revisiting both the highs and lows that have shaped my path, I discovered a new energy and pride for the achievements I have accomplished. The act of writing itself was almost cathartic, helping me make sense of everything I've experienced, learned, and overcome.

I started with my notebook, then transferred it to a Word document, but I was struggling with the formatting, which kept jumping around, it was doing my little head in!

Once I discovered Bookmagic.ai it very quickly became easy. This software has been a key element in completing the manuscript and the speed at which I've done it. Logging on each time was a pleasure and I was excited to write the next chapter.

Now, I know some of you might be put off by the mere mention of AI, but let me assure you, the words are entirely mine. What it does do though is assist in structuring your content, organising your thoughts, and keeping an eye on essential details like word count and pacing. It doesn't write the book for you, but it offers a set of tools that makes the writing process more seamless and efficient.

For someone like me, juggling multiple projects while also writing, it's been an absolute game-changer. With so many thoughts running through my mind, Bookmagic has helped me map out the structure of my chapters, ensuring I stayed on track and covered all the key points I wanted to share. It's not easy to put thirty-two years of experience into a book, and keeping that content focused and relevant was crucial. The platform provided just the right amount of guidance to help me stay organised while maintaining my voice throughout.

I highly recommend writing your story down, especially if you're someone who wants to share your knowledge and experiences but feels overwhelmed by the sheer volume of content or the organisation required.

Ultimately, this book has been a reflection of my journey, and the process of writing it has only deepened my appreciation for everything I've learned over the years. I don't think it will be my last!

Go on... what are you waiting for?

Co-Piloting 2025

Finding my thing

When I first read Daniel Priestley's *Key Person of Influence*, one recurring statement stood out. He talked throughout the book about discovering your theme. There was no grand reveal at the end of the book, no step-by-step formula to solve the conundrum. Instead, he advised that if you hadn't figured it out yet, you should read the book again, and again, until you did.

I was intrigued.

As I read, I kept asking myself: What is my thing? What's the common thread running through my life and career?

And, as you've probably guessed, the answer eventually came to me, just as I knew it would.

The moment of clarity

It was mid-2024, and I was sitting in a coffee shop (my favourite place to write) in my old hometown of King's Lynn, armed with my trusty notebook and pen (my favourite writing tools).

The cafe was busy, and an unsettled baby nearby was creating a bit of a distraction, but I was deep in creative flow. I let the words spill onto the page, no filter, no structure, just writing freely in an attempt to untangle my thoughts.

At the beginning of this book, in the section called Who Am I?, there's a line that reads:

"I prefer being second-in-command to first."

At first, I questioned it.

As a former business owner with an entrepreneurial mindset, was that really true? But the idea had surfaced that day for a reason, and I felt compelled to explore it further.

The role I was meant for

Looking back over my career, I have realised that in most cases, I've been second-in-command.

- In my family, we followed my dad's vision for business success.
- I worked alongside my husband.
- I supported the owner of Cloud Bookkeeping.
- I partnered with Richie Finney MBE at Captain Fawcett.
- More recently, I've been Richard Hoole's right hand at ASC Metals Lincoln.

In each of those roles, I've sat in the First Officer's seat, right next to the Captain, co-piloting the plane to their chosen destination.

I have been the supporter, confidante, and Swiss army knife. I have taken the pilot's seat when the Captain needed to step away, and I have carried out my role with integrity, precision, and alignment with the journey we were on.

I have taken business owners who were stuck on the runway, helped them refuel and then sat with them to take off into the skies. I have helped lead their crews, ensuring they were happy, trained, and fully on board with the mission.

And in that moment, sitting in that cafe, it hit me:

I am a Co-Pilot. That's my thing.

Why every business owner needs a Co-Pilot

Many business owners are in the pilot seat. They have their passengers (customers) on board and a crew (team) helping to serve them. They know their destination, have a flight plan, and an ETA. But what many don't have is a Co-Pilot, someone who understands the mission, anticipates turbulence, and supports them every step of the way.

And let's be honest, can a plane even take off without both a Captain and a First Officer? I don't think so. A Co-Pilot is essential.

Go find your thing

Through the process of writing this book and learning from others who've walked similar paths, I've discovered my theme. I've only ever wanted to achieve my absolute full potential and I think I'm now on my way!

I hope that by reading this book, you've taken away some tips, some do's, some definite don'ts, or maybe even something bigger.

Whatever it is, I hope I've inspired you to find your thing, go all in, and absolutely smash it.

I'll be cheering for you and guiding you from the sidelines.

Go reach your own full potential!

Thanks To

Asha Clearwater – Of Turquoise Tiger, thank you for setting me on this writing journey.

Mark Beaumont-Thomas – Of Lexicon Marketing, for being the eagle-eyed editor throughout this nerve-wracking task of getting my first book right.

Simon Clements – For the wonderful cover design that adorns this book.

Toby Lee – For the best photoshoot I've ever done and the images we captured that day.

Nat Ravenlock – For typesetting this book and making the process so easy.

Gary Turner – For bringing Xero to the UK.

Croz Crossley – For telling me to relax, and then relax again and hey, I almost forgot… relax some more!

Nina Goel – A random meeting at York Races in 2024 that has led to a beautiful friendship, thank you for being there at that moment.

Debbie Fogarty – For keeping my head straight all these years.

Jill McCulloch – For giving me a kick up the arse back in 2014.

Steve The Barman – For believing in me when I didn't believe in myself.

To every businessperson that was involved with my 4Networking teams – we did it together, thank you!

Anne-Marie Martin – For trusting me early on with your franchise when I started Athena.

My Athena Team – Martine Halls, Karen Hurn, Sarah Warden – you ladies rock!

The Crew at Captain Fawcett – it was a pleasure to work with you all. See the wonderful world of Captain Fawcett at captainfawcett.com.

Jim Clarke – Thank you for your sage advice and the first-class adventures, they were on another level.

Iain & Louise Crockart – for support, guidance and giggles.

Richard Finney MBE – Trains, Planes and Automobiles, we did them all and had the most amazing time! Thank you for trusting and believing in me.

The ASC Team – Thank you for trusting me; it's an honour to help lead your company. I respect and admire what each and every one of you brings to the business.

Richard Hoole – Thank you for allowing me to help you run the company your father founded. It is an honour and a privilege.

Brad Burton – Always available, always helpful, always ready to give me motivation when I need it, cheering me on and telling me to get back out there.

To Sep, Emma, Steve and Liz – Thank you all for your fabulous welcome, friendship and hospitality in my new home in Lincolnshire.

My good friends Tracey and Kim, for our mutual love of all things Italian, chats, giggles and support.

To Steve, for giving me Hannah.

To my sister Lisa, for being the chalk to my cheese! For the fabulous mother you are and aunty to my daughter.

To Mum for being the backbone behind the family enabling Dad to build his vision. I am so truly grateful for all you've done for us (and that I've inherited your love of cooking too!)

To Dad, you made such a lasting impact on us all and I aspire to continue making you proud, carrying on the family business legacy.

To my stepdaughter Ellie, for showing me nothing but kindness and love since we've been in each other's lives. Your life and adventures are only just beginning.

To Hannah, thank you for choosing me as your Mum. It is a true privilege to see you grow into the beautiful and strong woman I knew you were going to be when you were born. You, my darling, have this world at your feet.

And finally, to Keith, my life-partner in crime, thank you for taking me off the shelf, for keeping my feet on the ground, for being my sounding board and speaker of sense. I'm looking forward to where this life takes us both and the adventures we will share together. *All My Love, LL X*

Printed in Great Britain
by Amazon